CW01011302

Economics of Leisure

Ian Wilson
King's School, Macclesfield

Series Editor
Susan Grant
West Oxfordshire College

Heinemann Educational Publishers
Halley Court, Jordan Hill, Oxford OX2 8EJ
Part of Harcourt Education

Heinemann is the registered trademark of Harcourt Education Limited
© Harcourt Education, 2003

First published 2003

07 06 05 04 03 02
10 9 8 7 6 5 4 3 2 1

British Library Cataloguing in Publication Data is available
from the British Library on request.

ISBN 0 435 33045 4

Typeset by TechType, Abingdon, Oxon

Original illustrations © Harcourt Education Limited 2003

Cover design by Gecko Ltd

Printed in the UK by Biddles Ltd

Acknowledgements
The publishers would like to thank the following for permission to reproduce copyright
material:

Broadcasters' Audience Research Board for table on p39; Crown Copyright for the
tables on pp.33, 34, 35 ©Crown Copyright material is reproduced under Class Licence
number C01W00141 with the permission of the Controller of HMSO and the Queen's
Printer for Scotland; *The Economist* for the extract on p80 ©*The Economist Newspaper
Limited*, London (10/11/01); *The Guardian* for the extracts on p10 (28/08/00) ©*The
Guardian*; p29 (18/10/02) ©*The Guardian*/Andrew Clark; p75 (07/10/02) ©*The
Guardian*/Dan Milmo; p78 (26/03/02) ©*The Guardian*/Greg Ward; p86 (24/08/02)
©*The Guardian*; p84 (04/06/02) ©*The Guardian*/Andrew Clark; p90 (21/08/01) ©*The
Guardian*/Tony Grayling; p96 (18/08/01) ©*The Guardian*/Owen Boycott; KeyNote
Limited for table on p36; *The Observer* for the extracts on p18 (13/01/02) ©*The
Observer*/Joanna Walters; p42 (13/01/02) ©*The Observer*/Heather Cannon; p72
(24/03/02) ©*The Observer*/Nick Mathiason; p85 (07/10/01) ©*The Observer*; p62
(03/03/02) ©*The Mail on Sunday*/Rachel Unsworth.

Every effort has been made to contact copyright holders of material reproduced in this
book. Any omissions will be rectified in subsequent printings if notice is given to the
publishers.

Contents

Preface

This new book is a very welcome addition to the *Studies in Economics and Business* series. It applies relevant economic concepts to the key issues involved in the leisure sector in a clear and challenging way.

The book should prove to be a valuable resource for people studying for:

- OCR's A2 module 2884, 'Economics of Work and Leisure'
- AQA's AS module 3, 'Markets at Work'.

The author is an experienced teacher at King's School, Macclesfield, and a Principal Examiner with a major examining board.

Susan Grant
Series Editor

Introduction

The book aims primarily to assist students and teachers as they prepare for OCR's A2 module 2884, 'Economics of Work and Leisure', although it is hoped that the text will also be of relevance to students preparing for AQA's AS module 3, 'Markets at Work', and other A level students taking microeconomic courses.

Chapter 1 addresses the question of the meaning of leisure in an economic context, with particular emphasis on the relationship between leisure and work, and on leisure as a 'product'.

Chapter 2 outlines the major 'industries' which make up the supply of leisure services, the three sectors that supply them, and the concept of elasticity of supply.

Chapter 3 considers the demand for leisure products, with its main emphasis on elasticities of demand.

Chapter 4 provides some data on the UK leisure sector, both in total and for some selected parts of it.

Chapter 5 first provides an explanation of the economists' theory of market structures at a level suitable for all A level students, and then puts forward suggestions for its relevance to some particular leisure industries.

Chapter 6 considers leisure in a macroeconomic context. The leisure sector has an impact on the national economy, and is itself affected by changes in macroeconomic variables. There is also recognition of an environmental dimension to leisure activities.

All books in this series follow a similar format, which includes end-of-chapter data response questions. In this volume, however, there are rather more of these than is usual, and they play a more central role. As in the other books, they aim to give students practice at answering a type of question set in end-of-course public examinations. There are two further reasons, however, for including so many of them in the form that they appear:

- Students are not required by the examination boards to have large amounts of detailed factual knowledge of all possible leisure industries; that would be an absurd requirement. Rather, they are expected to be able to apply their understanding of the appropriate economic concepts and theories to leisure industries, and to ongoing developments in them. Much of the up-to-date information on such developments is most easily accessible in newspapers. Thus, the data response questions are all in the form of adapted newspaper articles, and they form an important complement to the text, as well as a means of enabling students to test their understanding of it. The fact that most of the articles in this book are from *The Guardian* or *The Observer* merely reflects the newspaper reading habits of the author! Teachers will no doubt find articles which can provide the basis for equally valid questions in other publications.

- Teachers will be able to use the format and structure of the questions provided to devise their own, and thereby help students to update their awareness of future developments in leisure industries.

To emphasize these roles, data response questions are included not only at the end of each chapter, but also as a set in *Chapter 7*.

Chapter One

The meaning of leisure

'*Work expands so as to fill the time available for its completion.*'
C. Northcote Parkinson, *Parkinson's Law*

Introduction

What is 'leisure'? Is it a *product*, in a similar category to goods like apples, or services like hairdressing? If so, an economist can presumably analyse the market for leisure in the same way as the market for apples or for hairdressing. The price of the 'product', and the quantities of it consumed or produced, could be explained as resulting from the interaction between individuals, who derive satisfaction from consuming it, and firms, who derive profit (or whatever other objectives they may pursue) from producing it.

Alternatively, is leisure really a *process*? To the vast numbers of individuals who, in everyday language, 'work for a living', leisure is the time that they spend not in work, and what they do during that time. If this is a better interpretation, then an economist's analysis of leisure should be in terms of the choice that is made between spending time at work, earning income, and leisure time, and then of the choices which are made about how to use this leisure time.

In practice, of course, any attempt to analyse the economics of leisure must take both of these interpretations into account, and must also recognize that there are many complications and complexities within each. Not all 'leisure' products involve a direct monetary cost to the consumer: a walk in the countryside, sunbathing on a beach, or digging the garden, for example. Analysis of the demand for such 'products' is therefore likely to be rather different from the analysis of demand for apples, or for the services of a hairdresser, which involve payment of a price to a seller. Also, not all individuals are workers; many are retired, some are unemployed. They don't conform exactly to the analysis of leisure as the process of choosing not to work.

It is already clear that leisure is not a simple economic variable: if it were, it would not merit a whole A level book to itself! Everyone knows when they are enjoying leisure and values it, though perhaps we should exclude so-called 'workaholics' from this! However its meaning is by no means clear-cut.

Leisure and opportunity cost

Let us first outline the traditional economist's analysis of leisure as being the process of choosing not to spend time at work. Individuals in the labour market can choose, to a greater or lesser degree, the number of hours they work. The decision to take off a potential hour of work-time, to spend it 'at leisure', is an economic choice, and has an **opportunity cost**. The worker is giving up an hour's pay to gain an hour of leisure. The hourly wage represents the opportunity cost of the hour of leisure. This is illustrated in Figure 1.

On the y-axis, A represents the maximum number of hours available to the worker per time period – per week, say – to be allocated between time at work and time at leisure. This will be less than 168 hours (7 days at 24 hours per day) by the amount of time taken up by necessary activities which can be classified as neither work nor leisure, for example sleeping, eating and washing. (This is sometimes referred to as **maintenance time.**)

On the x-axis, N represents the maximum amount of weekly income from work available to the worker; it will equal A multiplied by the worker's hourly wage-rate.

The line NA, then, represents all combinations of leisure time and income that are available to the worker. The worker may choose a high level of weekly income (N_1) but will then have only A_1 hours of leisure available. On the other hand, a low level of income (N_2) may be chosen, with much more leisure time available (A_2).

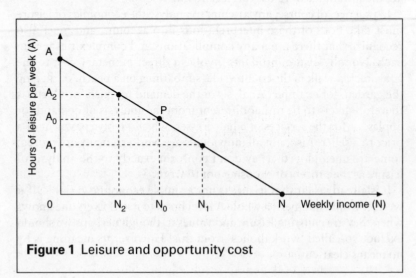

Figure 1 Leisure and opportunity cost

For any given worker, given his or her preferences, there will be a particular combination of income and leisure on the line NA which yields greatest **satisfaction/utility**, for example at point P, the choice of N_0 income and A_0 leisure per week.

It is instructive to consider how this decision may be affected by a change in the worker's hourly wage-rate. (This analysis, in fact, forms the basis of the economist's explanation of the **short-period supply of labour**.) Suppose the hourly wage rate increases by 10 per cent. In Figure 2, this means that N′ (N + 10 per cent of N) is the new, greater, available income, and N′A therefore represents the new, better, set of combinations of income and leisure available to the worker. The worker will then choose a different combination of the two, and be able thereby to gain a greater level of satisfaction.

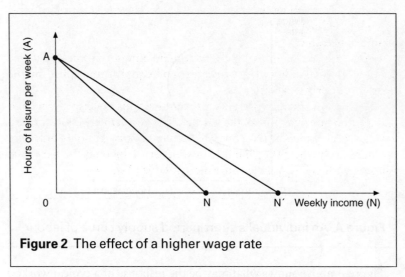

Figure 2 The effect of a higher wage rate

Precisely what new combination the worker will choose will depend on how he or she values two notionally different impacts of the rise in the hourly wage. These are as follows.

- The greater hourly wage means that leisure is more expensive for the worker; it now has a 10 per cent greater opportunity cost. This would lead the worker to choose to work more hours, choosing less of the more expensive leisure time. This is called a **substitution effect**.
- On the other hand, the greater hourly wage also means that the worker is better off, and so will choose to 'consume' more of those

5

'products' which yield positive satisfaction, of which leisure is certainly one. This is called an **income effect**.

Thus, the overall effect of the change depends on which of these two effects predominates. If, for a particular worker, the substitution effect is greater than the income effect, the outcome will be a decision to work more hours, and so enjoy fewer hours of leisure. On the other hand, another worker may place a greater priority on leisure. His or her preferences would imply that the income effect of the rise in hourly wage rate is greater than the substitution effect, resulting in a decision to work fewer hours, and benefit from the wage rise by enjoying increased leisure time.

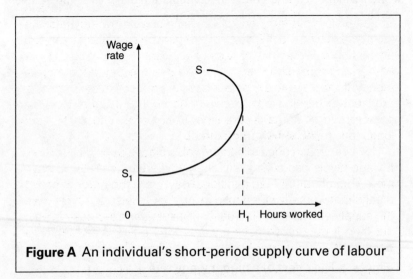

Figure A An individual's short-period supply curve of labour

Figure A above shows what may be the response of a typical worker to increases in the hourly wage-rate; this is explained further in the box below. S_1 is the wage below which no labour will be supplied. This could correspond to the kind of benefit levels a person might expect to receive if they were unemployed. The worker is prepared to increase the hours offered for work up to a maximum of H_1. After this the worker would choose to work fewer hours.

This analysis makes the assumption that it is the wage rate which alone determines the supply of labour and that all other factors remain unchanged. In fact it is more complicated than this. The amount a person is prepared to work is also tied up with what makes a person motivated to work. This can be affected by such things as the recognition given, the teamwork or promotion prospects available and the amount of job satisfaction. The level of taxation may also be important.

Incentives to work: the income effect and the substitution effect

The backward sloping supply curve

Generally people might be expected to increase the amount of labour they were prepared to supply as wage rates rise. Work and leisure can be regarded as substitutes for each other. Changes in wage levels will affect people's choices about how they allocate their time. If wage levels rise, people may be encouraged to work longer hours. Higher pay provides the incentive for people to work harder and most firms recognize the need to pay people more money if they are to be persuaded to work overtime. Here the prospect of earning a higher wage is enough to persuade the person to forgo some leisure time. People may choose to work longer due to the **substitution effect.**

However, much depends on the value placed upon leisure time. If wage levels rise sufficiently, then workers may prefer to have more time off rather than additional pay. Here the **income effect** means that workers will choose to 'buy' more leisure. In this case the supply of labour will increase initially with an increase in pay, but then it may move back towards the vertical axis forming a **backward sloping supply curve** as shown in Figure A.

Source: Adapted from *Core Economics*, EBEA, Heinemann, 1995.

Applications

The above analysis has a number of interesting applications. One of these relates to how a group of workers in an occupation, or employed by a firm, will respond to a change in the relevant wage-rate. Would the effect of, say, a 10 per cent rise in hourly pay result in, for example, A level examiners choosing to offer to work more hours, or to take the opportunity to enjoy more leisure time? The latter would presumably not be the outcome intended by the examination boards!

A second case where the choice between income and leisure has important practical consequences concerns the response of workers to a change in the marginal rate of income taxation. Suppose, for example, that a government reduces the standard rate of income tax by 1p in the pound. In effect, this represents an increase in the take-home rate of pay of workers who pay tax, so that they may choose to work more or fewer hours, dependent, as discussed above, on the workers' preferences. From time to time, such a policy has been proposed, largely on the grounds that it would give greater 'incentives' to workers. Presumably the proponents do not have in mind the incentive to enjoy more leisure.

Leisure as a product

The essence of the way economists look at the demand for a product is consideration of the benefit, or satisfaction, or utility that is gained from consuming it. This can clearly be applied in the traditional way to an explanation of consumer demand for individual leisure activities.

For example, when a household is deciding what form of summer holiday to take, or whether or not to take out family membership for a local fitness centre, the decision can be analysed in terms of the perceived benefit compared to the price. Similarly, decisions about how to spend money allocated to leisure activities involve, to the economist, allocating expenditure to different options in such a way as to maximize total satisfaction. This is in principle achieved when the addition to satisfaction gained from the last unit of expenditure is the same for each option under consideration.

Let us move on to consider supply. The firms providing leisure activities will make decisions about the volume of the product to supply to the market, and its price, by considering:

- their objectives
- the demand for the product
- the costs of providing it.

This applies to firms selling package holidays and to personal fitness trainers – both in the **private sector** – and also to **public sector** provision of museums or public library lending services. In addition, the market structure in which the firm operates – the extent to which the market is contestable, for example – will also have an impact on prices and output.

Such influences, as well as those on demand for leisure products, are considered in detail in later chapters.

What is a contestable market?

'Contestable markets' is a recent theory of market structure which is based on the likely effect which potential new entrants could have on the price and output decisions of firms already in the market (**incumbent firms**).

A *contestable market* is a market structure in which entry into an industry is free and exit is costless. Even the *threat* of new firm entry causes incumbent firms to act as though such potential entry actually exists. Instead of regarding competitive behaviour as existing only in a perfectly or monopolistically competitive market, it could exist in markets which are contestable.

The notion of contestability was developed by the American economist William Baumol. He considered the case of an unregulated airline route. Even if an airline operator were the only one on a particular route it would not be able to charge excessive fares. If it did, new operators would enter the market. There would be no irrecoverable costs, because new operations can lease their aircraft. Even if they were purchased, they could still be sold if the operator decided to leave the market.

Like perfect competion, and to a certain extent monopoly, contestable markets are not so much a description of the real world but rather a benchmark against which other theories of market behaviour can be assessed.

Source: *Business Economics* by A. Griffiths and S. Ison, Heinemann, 2001.

Leisure and spending

The point has been made earlier that not all leisure involves spending money. Digging the garden – or even just contemplating it – is described by many in the UK as a major pastime whenever surveys of use of leisure time are reported. Many other leisure activities do require expenditure by those who 'consume' them, however.

The range of activities that can be included within the category 'leisure' is extremely wide. Travel and tourism represents one very large area of activity, and expenditure. Sport, in its broadest interpretation, with consumers both as participants and as spectators, is another, and there are many, many more. Using computers and watching television occupy, for many people, many hours of leisure time. The arts – including music, theatre, film and fine art – represent a top priority in the use of leisure time for some, and hold a degree for interest for many more. Then there are a whole range of pastimes, such as angling, ornithology and rambling, that are highly valued as leisure time pursuits by many. They all generate satisfaction to their consumers, and virtually all involve spending money, since often the necessary equipment (e.g. binoculars and bird guides for ornithologists) involves expenditure, and travel is involved, even if there is no direct spending needed to undertake the activity itself.

Because of the huge – and, with increasing affluence, growing – expenditure on leisure activities in an advanced economy such as the UK, the relationships between leisure and the national economy are important ones. These relationships are very much two-way.

- Leisure spending has a significant influence on macroeconomic variables such as employment/unemployment and the balance of overseas payments.
- Government macroeconomic policy changes in, for example, taxes or interest rates have significant impacts on the leisure sector of the economy.
- Leisure activity – the most obvious aspect, perhaps, being tourism – has important impacts on the domestic and international environment, and on the UK as a member of the European Union.

These issues are considered further in later chapters.

KEY WORDS

Opportunity cost	Income effect
Maintenance time	Backward sloping supply curve
Satisfaction/utility	Private sector
Short-period supply of labour	Public sector
Substitution effect	

Further reading

Atkinson, A., Unit 1 in *Economics*, 3rd edn, Causeway Press, 2000.

Hale, G., Chapter 1 in *Labour Markets*, Heinemann Educational, 2001.

Tribe, J., *The Economics of Leisure and Tourism*, 2nd edn, Butterworth–Heinemann, 1999.

Useful website

- Please go to www.heinemann.co.uk/hotlinks and enter the code 04545.

Essay topics

a) Explain why the short-period supply curve to an occupation may be backward-sloping. [10]
b) Discuss the possible effects of a rise in the UK's standard rate of income tax. [15]

Data response question

This task is based on a question set by OCR in June 2002. Read the piece 'Give us a break', which is adapted from the *The Guardian* of 28 August 2000. Then answer the questions.

Give us a break

Although a recent poll showed strong support for three extra bank holidays in Britain to bring the country into line with the rest of Europe, the same report put the figure for those workers not using their full entitlement to paid holidays as high as 25 per cent. The four weeks' annual holiday now guaranteed to us by European law is for some, by their own choice, being reduced to three or even two – much to the satisfaction of the Institute of Directors, which has long grumbled about the amount of time British employees have off work.

Similar trends are seen in other major world economies. In the USA, there has been a reduction of leisure time for the average worker of 140 hours a year over the past 20 years, and one in three Americans take half or less of their already low holiday entitlement. In Japan, workers on average now take only 9.5 of their 17 days' statutory holiday entitlement.

Table A gives some relevant comparative data on hours worked and holiday entitlement.

Table A The working week and annual holiday entitlement in selected countries, 1999

	Britain	France	Germany	Italy	USA
Average working week (hours)	43.2	39.7	39.9	38.1	N/A
Annual public holidays (days)	8	11	14	16	9
Annual paid holiday entitlement, excluding public holidays (days)	28	N/A	37	42	12

Note: N/A indicates data not available.

The tendency towards increased hours worked raises output and leads to rewards being taken in the form of higher pay rather than increased leisure time.

A number of reasons are given for a rise in average hours worked:

- decline of trade union influence
- introduction of new technology
- economic globalization, leading to more people working across time zones.

There is no likelihood that such reasons will cease to operate and so leisure time seems likely to continue to be squeezed in the future.

1. Using Table A, compare the time spent at work by the average worker in Britain and in Germany. [2 marks]
2. From the information provided, identify *two* pieces of evidence which support the case that workers in the USA put a relatively low value on leisure time. [2 marks]
3. Average earnings in Italy are greater than in Britain despite the fact that Italian workers spend less time at work. State and explain *two* reasons that economists might give to explain this. [4 marks]
4. (a) Explain what is meant by the opportunity cost of leisure. [2 marks]

   (b) As noted in the information given, many workers in the advanced economies are taking less holiday than their entitlement. Explain what this behaviour of these workers might indicate about their attitude to the trade-off between work and leisure. [4 marks]
5. Discuss the view offered towards the end of the piece that 'leisure time seems likely to continue to be squeezed in the future'. [6 marks]

Chapter Two

Characteristics of leisure industries

'*All intellectual improvement arises from leisure.*'
Samuel Johnson, quoted in Boswell's *Life of Johnson*, vol. ii

Introduction

The point has been made in the previous chapter that leisure is not a simple economic variable, and it is equally the case that it is not easy to produce an exhaustive list of what constitutes a leisure industry, or the leisure sector of the economy.

Some 'production' is unambiguously part of it: a theatre play or a professional sporting event, a family weekend break at a hotel or a trip to a hiker's pub in the Lake District, an afternoon at a museum or a local authority leisure centre, the sale of a cricket bat or a package holiday for two on a Greek island.

On the other hand, a working lunch at a restaurant, an A level Biology group's visit to the Natural History Museum, a business flight to Athens, whilst all using resources which are usually categorized as amongst those allocated within the 'leisure sector' of the economy, are clearly not parts of leisure spending.

Nevertheless, the entries in Table 1 would be generally acceptable as a summary of broad categories making up most of the demand for (and expenditure on) leisure, and the associated suppliers.

Table 1 Broad categories of leisure

Type of demand/expenditure	Leisure sector suppliers
Entertainment (events)	Professional sports, cinema, theatre, concerts, television and radio
Entertainment (eating out)	Restaurants, clubs, bars
Holidays	Travel agents, hotels, airlines, rail operators
Hobbies/pastimes	Leisure centres, voluntary clubs, clothing and equipment suppliers

Sectors supplying leisure

Whereas many products are universally supplied by the private sector of the economy, by firms whose primary motivation is to generate profit for their owners (usually shareholders), this is not the case within the 'leisure industry'. Whilst there are many private sector firms providing leisure services, there is also significant provision both by public sector organizations and by the **voluntary sector**. Let us briefly consider each.

Private sector

Of the four categories identified in Table 1, in the UK the whole of the holidays segment and 'eating out' entertainment, clothing and equipment suppliers and some other areas of hobbies and pastimes (e.g. private health/gym clubs), and much of 'events' entertainment, are provided by private sector firms. They collect together factors of production for payment, sell their goods or services to generate revenue, and aim to make profit as the difference between revenues and costs. (Chapters 3 and 5 attempt to analyse their behaviour in more detail.) Some private sector firms are very large concerns. See Box 3.

Sport as a brand

Many sports franchises are now very big brands, generating millions of pounds of revenue each year. These include UK football clubs, American football teams and formula one teams. The most valuable sports brand is currently Dallas Cowboys football team. The team's brand value is immense, with the club selling everything from shirts to duvets. The most valuable sports brand in Europe is Manchester United, a club with a world-wide fan base.

Public sector

The public sector, or governmental, involvement in the provision of leisure services takes two forms. One is direct; public ownership of the BBC, for example, or local authority provision of leisure centres and public libraries. The other is through **subsidies**, whereby the government gives financial help to organizations such as the Welsh National Opera or local theatres.

The obvious question is why a government should choose to be so involved. The answer lies in two concepts used by economists; **merit goods**, and **positive externalities**.

- A merit good is one that, in the government's view, generates more benefit for consumers than they realize, so that consumption of merit goods would be lower than is socially optimal if their provision were left to the free market. The examples most commonly given are health and education; but in this context, one would include such leisure provision as museums and public libraries.

- Positive externalities arise when the provision of a good or service generates beneficial consequences to third parties who are not directly involved in the original transaction. For example, an individual might be a more productive employee if he or she is a regular user of a local leisure centre.

There are, inevitably, debates about what precisely does or does not constitute a merit good, and what level of benefit or positive externality is generated. Suffice it to say that these are the economic grounds on which public sector provision or subsidization of some leisure services is justified.

Voluntary sector

This third sector is particularly a feature of the 'leisure industry', and takes a multitude of forms; amateur dramatic societies, amateur sports clubs, brass bands, bridge clubs, bird-watching societies, and so on. Their legal status also varies, for example many are registered charities. What they have in common, in essence, is that they provide leisure interests for their participants.

Comment

Both public and voluntary sector organizations face costs, and therefore need to generate revenues, just as do private sector leisure industry firms. The difference, though, is that their objectives – and often the source of their revenues – are different.

In the case of public sector provision, the objective tends to be maximum 'consumption', subject to the need to operate within the financial constraints imposed. This is not to deny the relevance of economic considerations, of course; one only has to recall the debate about whether or not there should be a charge levied for visits to museums or art galleries.

For voluntary sector organizations, objectives are probably more varied; for example, the provision of opportunities and facilities for the existing membership, expansion of membership, or the attraction of an 'audience', where relevant. Again, though, there are economic considerations involved, for example, there is generally an inverse relationship between size of membership and joining subscriptions.

It is also worth pointing out that, with the development in the UK of National Lottery funding opportunities for voluntary sector organizations, in effect some differences between the public sector and the voluntary sector have become blurred.

Elasticity of supply

An important aspect of the supply of any good or service is the extent to which it responds to changed circumstances, for example in technology or, most importantly, in demand.

In the case of voluntary and perhaps public sector leisure services, such response tends to be fairly straightforward and direct; demand tends to create its own supply. Thus, after an Olympic Games has generated TV coverage of gymnastics, there tends to be an increased demand to take up and practise the sport, and local authority leisure centres and voluntary clubs increase their provision in response.

Of broader relevance is the nature of the response of supply when demand changes are reflected through a free market, via price. Economists use the concept of **price elasticity of supply** (PES) to measure the extent of the response. PES is defined as:

$$\frac{\text{percentage change in quantity supplied}}{\text{percentage change in price}}$$

and is characterized as 'elastic or 'inelastic' according to whether the value of PES in a particular industry is greater or less than 1, respectively. A couple of hypothetical examples will illustrate some of the important issues involved.

Example 1

Suppose that, over a period of increasing affluence, increased demand in the UK for holidays in the Caribbean results in a 20 per cent rise in their price. In the short run there are two possible outcomes.

- There is no spare capacity amongst tour operators, hotels or airlines. Supply would therefore be unchanged, and PES = 0%/20% = 0.
- With plenty of spare capacity, tour operators increase the number of holidays available by 40 per cent, so that PES = 40%/20% = 2.

In both cases, however, it may be that long-run supply will change in a different way. For example, particularly if the rise in demand is expected to be a permanent phenomenon, suppliers are likely to consider investment in additional facilities – hotels, air flights – and so increase their supply, or increase it further, in the long run.

Thus, PES is likely to be greater, the longer the time period under consideration; and greater in the short run, the more there exists spare capacity.

Example 2

Suppose that a successful TV series on the subject of chess has the effect of significantly increasing the demand to play chess as a pastime. One would expect local chess clubs to be affected to some extent, and they would simply increase their membership, as voluntary sector organizations. However, there would also be a rise in demand – and so, in a free market, price – for commercially manufactured chess sets.

Suppose, again, the prices of chess sets were to rise in the short run by 20 per cent. The extent of the resulting response in supply – and so the PES – might depend on the structure of the industry producing chess sets. If it is highly monopolistic, the dominant firm(s) may choose to limit the extra output produced to keep prices high, to maximize profits. On the other hand, if the industry is more contestable, with entry easy for new firms, or if it already consists of several fiercely competitive firms, then PES is likely to be much greater.

The issue of market structure is the subject of Chapter 5.

KEY WORDS

Voluntary sector	Positive externalities
Subsidies	Price elasticity of supply
Merit goods	

Further reading

Bamford, C., and Munday, S., Chapter 4 in *Markets*, Heinemann Educational, 2002.

Grant, S., and Vidler, C., Part 1 unit 30 in *Economics in Context*, Heinemann Educational, 2000.

Tribe, J., *The Economics of Leisure and Tourism*, 2nd edn, Butterworth–Heinemann, 1999.

Useful website
• Department of Trade and Industry: please go to www.heinemann. co.uk/hotlinks and enter code 04545S.

Essay topics
1. Discuss the cases for and against charging for admission to publicly funded museums and art galleries. [25]
2. Discuss the view that, if state subsidies are given to the Royal Ballet, they should go also to Wakefield Trinity Rugby League Football Club. [25]

Data response question
The following piece is adapted from an article in *The Observer* of 13 January 2002.

Newcomers buy jets as rivals stall

If one company's crisis is another's opportunity, the low-cost airlines are having a ball. The UK airline establishment is struggling to deal with the transatlantic economic downturn and the collapse in business travel since 11 September.

But as British Airways, Virgin Atlantic and BMI British Midland squirm in the tough financial climate, the likes of Easyjet, Ryanair and Go are revelling in their rivals' hard times.

They are expanding, building profits and handling more traffic. Easyjet last week announced plans to buy 75 new aircraft and increase its fleet almost fourfold to 90 planes by 2007, with the intention of running the fourth-biggest operation in Europe behind BA, Air France and Lufthansa.

Easyjet, whose main base is at Luton, and the Stansted-based Ryanair each carried 7 million passengers last year, more than BMI British Midland or Irish flag-carrier Aer Lingus. They are raising their passenger numbers at a rate of around 35 per cent a year, and City observers expect this to continue for the foreseeable future.

One transport analyst said this weekend: 'The cost of buying aircraft is down about 30 per cent and passenger volumes are above budget. Although fares have dropped to get people on board, the return on capital for airlines like Easyjet is rising.'

Ryanair is shopping for up to 50 bargain-priced second-hand Boeing 737s and has launched a new base in little-known Charleroi airport, near Brussels. It is forecast to make $100 million profit in the year to 31 March, up from around £80 million last year.

And Easyjet wants to expand out of Gatwick and is talking of establishing bases in Paris and Frankfurt. City forecasts put its profits for 2001–2002 at around £55m, up from £40m last time.

British Airways, meanwhile, is predicted to be bracing itself for a loss of almost £600m in 2001/02.

Roger Tejwani, analyst at WestLB Panmure, said that in the 1990s low-cost airlines built their traffic by expanding the market, attracting people to fly for the first time or fly more often.

Now they are moving increasingly into stealing market share, as larger carriers give in on loss-making routes and cut back frequencies, and business travellers switch over to the cheaper fares and 'no-frills' service as the economic outlook remains uncertain.

Tejwani said that around 14 per cent of the air market between the UK and the rest of Europe was now served by the low-cost airlines, compared with only around 4 per cent on the Continent. Observers believe there is huge scope for the young pretenders to grab much more of the market.

A fifth of US domestic fliers use the low-cost carriers, with the market dominated by Dallas-based Southwest Airlines.

Andrew Light, airline analyst at Schroder Salomon Smith Barney, said: 'The natural evolution of the short-haul market is towards the low-cost carrier, just as happened in the US 10 years ago, during the last downturn.'

It is becoming clear that the low-cost airlines are in many respects able to counter the gloomy economic cycle and are now prepared to exploit this by risking rapid expansion.

As one City expert concluded: 'If you are going to place a big order for aircraft now is the time. These guys are the future in Europe.'

Questions

1. The low-cost airlines are said to have used one strategy for first breaking into the airline market, and a different one for further expanding sales. Identify both strategies. [2 marks]
2. Explain how the comparisons made between the US and European airline markets suggest that there is scope for further massive growth in the future for firms such as Easyjet and Ryanair. [3 marks]
3. Explain the statement 'low-cost airlines are in many respects able to counter the gloomy economic cycle'. [4 marks]
4. Easyet has announced its intention of running the fourth-biggest operation in Europe by 2007. Discuss the possible implications for consumers and the airline industry of the fact that such changes in the structure of the industry are possible. [6 marks]

Chapter Three

The demand for leisure

'The thing which is the most outstanding and chiefly to be desired by all healthy and good and well-off persons is leisure with honour.'
Cicero, *Pro Sestio*

Introduction

The factors which influence the **demand** by consumers and potential consumers for leisure activities are no different from those underpinning the demand for any product. Demand can be defined as willingness and ability to buy, measured in units of the product per period of time.

The four main influences in general on the demand for any particular leisure activity are:

- its price
- consumer incomes
- the prices of other related products
- consumer preferences.

The importance of sport

Sport is becoming a major industry in the UK with spending on sport continuing to grow. In 2003 UK consumers were spending more than twice as much a year on sport as they were on going on holiday in the country.

Spending on most areas of sport is increasing with the biggest increase in spending being on pay television subscriptions. People are also spending more than twice as much on sports equipment than fifteen years ago. In terms of participation in sports, the most rapid growth has been in high cost areas such as gym membership.

Demand analysis

The economists' usual practice is to isolate the price of a product as the major influence on its demand. Assuming that all other influences remain unchanged – the *ceteris paribus* assumption beloved by all practitioners of the subject – then an individual consumer will respond to a change in the price of a product by changing in an inverse way the amount of it he or she demands. This is because of the principle of **diminishing marginal utility** – the more of a product the consumer consumes, the less highly he or she would value an additional unit of it – and the assumption that the consumer aims to maximize the total amount of satisfaction or utility which can be gained from expenditure on goods and services. Thus, a fall in the price of, say, visits to a cinema will mean that a consumer can gain more satisfaction from the same amount of spending per year on cinema visits than was previously the case. Rational behaviour will then mean that more annual cinema visits would increase the total satisfaction available to the consumer for the same total expenditure on all products.

An alternative way of looking at this – but one with the same conclusion – is through the ideas of income and substitution effects already encountered in Chapter 1. Thus, the fall in the price of cinema tickets will result in more annual cinema visits because:

- cinema visits are relatively cheaper than previously compared to the prices of alternatives, so resulting in a *substitution* of visits to the cinema for some of the alternatives
- the consumer has more real *income* as a result of the price fall, and some of it will be spent on more cinema visits.

What is true of one consumer is also true, by aggregation, of all consumers. So the **market demand curve** can be derived, showing the total number of visits to the cinema demanded per year, at all different possible prices; and because of the inverse relationship explained in the previous paragraph, it will be a downward-sloping line. It should be emphasized, though, that it will represent a valid statement of the relationship between amount demanded and price only *ceteris paribus*. If any of the other influences on demand change, then so will the demand curve.

Elementary analysis of **market equilibrium,** brought about as a result of the interaction of supply and demand influences, is then based partially on such a market demand curve. (More detailed consideration of supply influences is given in Chapters 4 and 5.) 'Equilibrium' occurs in any market when there exists no tendency for change to occur. This will be the case, as illustrated in Figure 3, when the price of cinema tickets is P, with Q visits to cinemas per year consumed and produced.

Similarly, whenever any of the relevant 'other influences' on demand change, elementary analysis will predict the resulting direction of

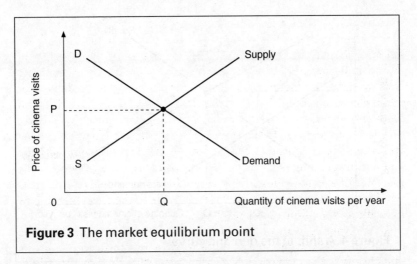

Figure 3 The market equilibrium point

change in price and quantity consumed. Whereas a change in supply will cause price to change, and as a result the quantity that consumers demand (in effect, a movement from one point to another *along* the demand curve), a change in any of the non-price influences on demand should be interpreted as causing a *shift* in the whole demand curve for the product, since it will cause a change in the quantity demanded at each possible price.

Extending the cinema visits illustration, one would expect, as shown in Figure 4, a shift to the right in the demand curve, and so a rise both in the equilibrium market price of cinema tickets and in the quantity consumed, if:

- consumers enjoy greater disposable income (assuming cinema visits to be a **normal good**; more consumed when consumers have more money to spend)
- the price of a **substitute good**, such as ten-pin bowling, increases,
- preferences change in favour of visits to the cinema, for example, as a result of an advertising campaign.

Elasticities

We have so far considered only the likely *direction* of change of price and quantity of a product as a result of changed circumstances. However, it is also important that the *sizes* of such changes be analysed. This requires looking at the *extent* to which demand responds to, or is sensitive to, changes in influencing variables. Economists do this through the use of the concept of **elasticity**.

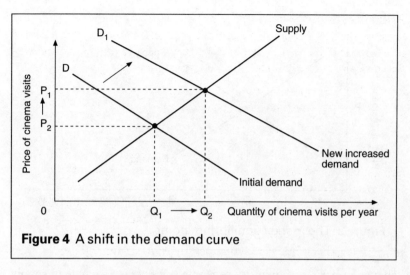

Figure 4 A shift in the demand curve

Elasticities of demand, then, measure the responsiveness of demand for a product to changes in an influencing variable.

They are calculated as:

$$\frac{\text{proportional change in demand}}{\text{proportional change in the influencing variable}}$$

Each elasticity has both a *sign* (positive or negative), which indicates the direction of the relationship involved, and a *size*, which measures the extent to which there is a relationship.

- If the relationship is quite a strong one, the numerical value of the elasticity will be greater than one, and the demand is said to be 'elastic' with respect to the variable concerned. This reflects the fact that the change in the influencing variable causes a proportionately greater change in demand.
- In contrast, a weaker relationship will give a value below one, and an 'inelastic' demand.

It is important here to emphasize that all elasticities are calculated on a ceteris paribus *basis. That is, it is assumed that all other factors that might influence the demand for the product are unchanged, so that it can reasonably be concluded that the change in demand is a result of the change in the one identified variable.*

It is perhaps best to illustrate the calculation of elasticities of demand through a series of hypothetical numerical examples. As emphasized above, each is calculated on a *ceteris paribus* basis.

Price elasticity of demand (PED)

Suppose that, as a result of a cut in the price of an annual season ticket to Macclesfield Town FC from £200 to £180, the number of tickets purchased rises from 500 to 510. The corresponding value of PED is

$$\frac{\text{proportional change in demand for tickets}}{\text{proportional change in the price}}$$

$$= (+10)/500 \text{ divided by } (-£20)/£200, \text{ which is } -0.2.$$

What can be concluded? The negative sign merely shows that price and quantity demanded are *inversely related*, which would be the case for virtually all products. The very low value of 0.2 indicates a highly price-inelastic demand for the product; the people of Macclesfield would be shown as very insensitive to price in their choice as between spending leisure time as a regular season-ticket supporter of their local football league club, or enjoying the other attractions offered by the town.

In general, one would expect the PED for leisure activities to be rather greater than in the above example. This is because the availability of close substitute products is the most important factor in determining PED, and for many leisure activities such substitutes clearly exist.

For example, the demand for mass tourism package holidays offered by different travel companies is known to be quite price-elastic; the companies certainly compete strongly on price. Similarly, the demand for starter packs offered by such organizations as the Royal Society for the Protection of Birds (RSPB) is quite price-elastic, as is the demand for relatively low-priced 'beginner' binoculars; in this market, there is quite strong competition among groups offering hobby activities to youngsters.

On the other hand, one would expect the demand for higher-priced, specialist binoculars to be much less price-elastic; potential purchasers (not dissimilar to Macclesfield Town soccer supporters, in this respect at least!) are extremely committed to ornithology as their leisure activity, and do not regard price as a particularly significant influence on their demand for associated products.

Income elasticity of demand (YED)

Suppose that, as a result of a rise in the average disposable incomes of UK households from £20 000 to £21 000 per annum, the yearly demand for weekend breaks with a particular hotel chain rose from 400 000 to 460 000. The corresponding value of YED is proportional change in demand for breaks

proportional change in disposable income

= (+60 000)/400 000 divided by (+£1000)/£20 000, which is +3.0.

The conclusion would be that demand for the product in question is quite strongly income-elastic (a 5 per cent rise in average disposable income resulting in a 15 per cent increase in demand), as well as that the product is 'normal', in the sense that its demand rises when income rises (i.e. YED is positive).

Since most leisure activities can be regarded as, in some sense, 'luxury' products, one would expect them to have relatively high income elasticities of demand, though there will certainly be considerable variations. The holiday market provides interesting examples.

Recent years, with growing affluence in the UK, have seen significant increases in demand for long-distance, expensive holidays, many of which have moved from niche products purchased by only a few in the direction of mass market destinations; the YED for such holidays will be greater than one. However, during the same period, demand for some traditional bottom-of-the-market package holidays has actually fallen; they have become **inferior products**, with a negative YED. Increased average incomes have resulted in lower demand for such holidays, as many consumers have opted for slightly more expensive packages which they regard as superior in quality.

Cross elasticity of demand (XED)

Suppose that, as a result of a fall in the average price of lunches at a local garden centre, from £5 to £4, there is an increase in weekly sales of the centre's bedding plants from 5000 to 5200. The corresponding value of XED is

proportional change in demand for plants

proportional change in the price of lunch

= (+200)/5000 divided by (−£1)/£5, which is −0.2.

Here, the sign reflects the nature of the relationship between the two products. It is a **complementary** relationship, in the sense that a fall in the lunch price would have resulted presumably in more visitors being attracted to the garden centre, who then purchased more bedding plants. As previously, though, the size of the XED is a measure of the degree of responsiveness; the demand for bedding plants is cross-inelastic with respect to the price of lunches, a 20 per cent cut in the latter resulting in only a 4 per cent increase in the former.

Whereas negative values for XED between two products reflect a complementary relationship between them, positive values mean that the products are substitutes. Thus, there will be a positive XED for Channel ferry crossings with respect to the price charged to cross by Eurostar; a fall (or rise) in the rail fare will lead to a fall (or rise, respectively) in the demand for ferry crossings.

The size of the coefficient reflects the closeness or otherwise of the relationship between the two products involved. This is the case whether the sign is positive or negative. As an example of positive values, the demand for one holiday company's fortnight package to Majorca in August will be quite highly cross-elastic with regard to the price of another's; a 5 per cent rise in the price of one would lead to a more than 5 per cent rise in demand for the other. On the other hand, the cross-elasticity of demand for Glasgow Rangers season tickets with respect to the price of the equivalent at Glasgow Celtic would be virtually zero; the clubs may be competitors in sporting terms, but, given the almost tribal loyalties associated with the support for the two clubs, there will be insignificant XED in terms of season ticket demand.

In the case of complements, the numerical example above illustrated a very cross-inelastic case. In contrast, the XED between overseas holidays and air flights will be much greater numerically, as well as being negative; a 10 per cent rise in air fares from the UK to California might well result in a greater than 10 per cent fall in UK demand for holidays there.

Other elasticities of demand
Although there is no direct measure of consumer preferences, the fourth of the major influences on demand, it is certainly possible to measure the responsiveness of demand for products to a range of factors which influence preferences. Two examples follow; in each case, as for other elasticities, the sign reflects the nature of the relationship, and the size its extent.

Example 1
Suppose – perhaps after the annual Wimbledon lawn tennis fortnight – that the Lawn Tennis Association (LTA) were to increase its expenditure on advertising the facilities and opportunities available at its affiliated local tennis clubs by 50 per cent, and the demand for club membership doubled. Then the corresponding advertising elasticity of demand is

proportional change in demand for membership

proportional change in advertising expenditure

= +100 per cent divided by +50 per cent, which is 2.0.

Example 2

Suppose that, after a drop in mean weekly temperature of 5 per cent in Devon holiday resorts, there was an increase of 4 per cent in the demand for use of the resorts' indoor swimming pools. Then the corresponding temperature elasticity of demand for the pools is

proportional change in demand for pools

proportional change in temperature

= 4 per cent divided by –5 per cent, which is –0.8.

Similar elasticities can be calculated for any factor which influences the demand for any leisure product.

Importance of elasticities

Detailed knowledge, to the extent that it is possible, of the various elasticities of demand, relating to the products that it sells is of immense value to any firm. In particular, firms have to make forecasts of the future demand for their products; the more accurately they forecast, indeed, the more successful they are likely to be. Knowledge of relevant elasticities makes forecasting very much more likely to be accurate.

The examples used in the previous section illustrate this well.

- Devon swimming pool owners will be able to obtain long- and short-range weather forecasts, and use knowledge of their temperature elasticity of demand to forecast use of their pools in forthcoming days and weeks.
- Knowledge of their advertising elasticity of demand will enable the Lawn Tennis Association to forecast, and therefore accurately plan to cater for, the increase in demand at its clubs which would result from its extra advertising.
- The garden centre, aware of the cross elasticity, could ensure it stocked up with the right amount of extra bedding plants in readiness for its reduction in lunch prices.
- Perhaps most usefully of all, the hotel chain can obtain forecasts of future trends in disposable incomes (produced by governments, as well as other economic forecasters), and so, with knowledge of appropriate income elasticities of demand, be able to predict its own future sales.

Accurate knowledge of price elasticity of demand is perhaps even more potentially beneficial to a firm because of the relationships between price changes, PED and the total revenue generated. If a product has price-inelastic demand, a rise in price will reduce demand to a proportionately smaller extent, so that total revenue generated will rise. Total profit will also increase, given that direct (variable) costs will also fall. On the other hand, a price cut when demand is price-elastic will also increase revenue, since sales increase proportionately more than the price is reduced; whether or not this results in increased profit depends on how much costs rise, relative to the increased revenue.

The great difficulty is that accurate knowledge of elasticities of demand is not easy to come by. There are basically two options for a firm.

- One is to try to use past data to estimate how demand has previously responded when other variables have changed. There are two problems with this approach. The first is that a change in sales is likely to have coincided with changes in more than one influencing variable; and the second is that, even if an accurate value for an elasticity is established, there can be no guarantee that it will apply exactly for a new change.
- The second method of attempting to estimate elasticities is through **market research**. Again, though, there are pitfalls, not to mention the expense involved. There is always a degree of uncertainty about how representative a sample is of the population from which it is drawn, and how much reliance can be placed on the results obtained.

In spite of these estimation difficulties, there is no doubt that for organizations providing leisure activities just as for others, decision-making in many areas is likely to be very much more successful if it is underpinned by knowledge of the various elasticities of demand that concern it. This is best demonstrated by the fact that firms expend a considerable amount of time, effort and money in their attempts to obtain relevant elasticity estimates.

> ## KEY WORDS
>
> | | |
> |---|---|
> | Demand | Elasticity |
> | Ceteris paribus | Price elasticity of demand |
> | Diminishing marginal utility | Income elasticity of demand |
> | Market demand curve | Inferior product |
> | Market equilibrium | Cross elasticity of demand |
> | Normal good | Complementary |
> | Substitute good | Market research |

Further reading

Bamford, C., and Munday, S., Chapters 2 and 3 in *Markets*, Heinemann Educational, 2002.

Gratton, C., and Taylor, P., *Economics of Sport and Recreation*, Spon Press, 2000.

Tribe, J., *The Economics of Leisure and Tourism*, 2nd edn, Butterworth–Heinemann, 1999.

Useful website

- Manchester United FC: please go to www.heinemann.co.uk/hotlinks and enter code 04545S.

Essay topics

a) Explain the meanings of price elasticity, income elasticity and cross elasticity of demand. [10]

b) Discuss the possible relevance to an up-market town centre restaurant of accurate knowledge of relevant elasticities of demand. [15]

Data response question

Read the following piece, which is adapted from a report in *The Guardian* on 18 October 2002. Then answer the questions that follow, using your knowledge of economic concepts.

Eurostar cuts fares

Eurostar has slashed the price of its flexible fares from London to Paris and Brussels in an attempt to reverse a steady decline in bookings. The Channel tunnel train company yesterday revealed that its passenger numbers had fallen for a fifth consecutive quarter. In an effort to turn round its fortunes, the company has cut its flexible return fares to its two main destinations from €300 to €200 in standard class, with a reduction from €400 to €300 in first class.

Eurostar's chief executive, Richard Brown, said: 'Business travel in particular is significantly down. Neither France, Britain nor Belgium is technically in recession, but business budgets are being cut substantially.'

Mr Brown denied suggestions from Eurotunnel, the tunnel's operator, that it was losing passengers to low-cost airlines.

1. Suppose that, as a result of the price cuts, passenger numbers increased by two-thirds in standard class and by 10 per cent in first class.
   (a) Calculate the two price elasticities of demand. [4 marks]
   (b) Identify the implications of each for Eurostar's total revenue. [6 marks]
2. Discuss the possible benefits to Eurostar of having accurate estimates of:
   (a) income elasticity of demand for its services [5 marks]
   (b) cross elasticity of demand between its services and those of low-cost airlines. [5 marks]

Chapter Four

Some trends in leisure industries

'The wisdom of a learned man cometh by opportunity of leisure; and he that hath little business shall become wise.'
The Bible, Ecclesiasticus 24

Introduction

This chapter follows on in particular from Chapter 2, with some data to give an indication of the size of, and trends in, the leisure sector within the UK economy, first in aggregate terms, and then in some (though by no means all) of the different segments.

It is important to recall the difficulties of definition which make the 'leisure sector' a somewhat slippery concept. It is also worth pointing out that several of the data response questions based on newspaper articles in this book give additional information on particular aspects of leisure industries.

The leisure sector in aggregate

The two most important measures of the size of an industry involve (a) the number employed within it, and (b) the value of expenditure on its products.

Employment

Table 1 shows estimates of the number of people employed in 1999 in different segments in the UK, with corresponding figures for 1989 and 1994 for comparison.

Table 1 Employment in the UK's leisure sector (thousands)

Segment	1989	1994	1999
Hotels and other accommodations	299	376	306
Restaurants, cafés etc.	283	372	358
Bars, pubs, clubs	428	399	429
Travel agents, tour operators	65	84	114
Libraries, museums etc.	83	77	85
Sport and other recreation	295	356	338
Total employees	1453	1664	1629
Estimate of self-employment	191	209	159

Source: ONS, *Annual Abstract of Statistics*, 2000

Note that while the hotel and restaurant figures will be overestimates of specifically leisure-related employment, the sport and recreation ones will be underestimates, and significant leisure-related transport employment is omitted.

Expenditure

The ONS website gives figures for average weekly household expenditure in the UK on leisure goods and services (Table 2).

Table 2 Average weekly household expenditure on leisure

	1990/91	2000/01
Total weekly expenditure of which:	£335.80	£385.70
Leisure goods and services	£44.60 (i.e. 13.3%)	£70.30 (i.e. 18.2%)

Note: The figures are given at constant 2000/01 prices; expenditure on fares, motoring, alcohol are not included.
Source: ONS website.

The same source – which incidentally begins with a comment that there is no universally agreed definition of what constitutes the leisure and recreation sector of the economy – gives data for total leisure spending in the UK (Table 3).

Table 3 Spending in the UK's leisure sector (£ billion)

	1995	1999	2004 (projected)
Leisure spending	118	154	196
As a percentage of total consumer expenditure	27.0	27.5	28.0

Note that these figures explicitly *include* spending on all media sources, reading, music at home, gardening and DIY, sports and fitness activities, catering outside the home, gambling, cinemas, theatres, music and the arts, tourist attractions, short-break holidays, but they *exclude* longer UK holidays and holidays overseas.

Comment

The employment data in Table 1 show persons employed in a relatively narrowly defined leisure sector, with significant growth during the

1990s. Weekly household expenditure, again fairly narrowly defined, grew quite dramatically during the 1990s according to Table 2, no doubt reflecting the fact that leisure spending takes an increasing share of spending as incomes increase. This trend is also shown in the total spending data in Table 3.

Particular segment – Tourism

Tables 4–6 show, respectively, total tourism in the UK, the numbers of holidays taken by UK residents, and visits abroad by UK residents, and to the UK by overseas residents.

Table 4 Statistics of total tourism in the UK

	1991	1999
Number of UK tourists (m)	76.0	123.3
Expenditure by UK tourists (£m)	7925	12915
Number of overseas tourists (m)	15.1	21.5
Expenditure by overseas tourists (£m)	6595	11030

Source: ONS, 2000.

Table 5 Number of holidays taken by UK residents (percentages)

	1978	1988	1998
No holidays	38	39	41
One holiday only	42	37	34
Two or more holidays	20	24	25
	100	100	100

Source: UK tourism survey. The figures include both domestic and foreign holidays, with a holiday being defined as four or more nights spent away from home.

Table 6 Visits abroad by UK residents, and to the UK by overseas residents (thousands of visits)

		1985	1999
Total visits overseas by UK residents	To W. Europe	18944	42762
	To N. America	914	4737
	To rest of world	1752	6342
Total visits to UK by overseas residents	From W. Europe	7870	16382
	From N. America	3797	4556
	From rest of world	2782	4530

Source: ONS, 2000.

Comment

Tables 4 and 6 show very significant increases over time in both numbers of tourists in the UK and number of visits both into and out of the UK, as well as rises in tourists' expenditures. Table 5 is perhaps more surprising, not so much in its demonstration of a growing number of UK residents taking more than one holiday per year, as the slight increase too in those taking no holidays.

Particular segment – Air travel

Table 7 shows various data for the UK air travel segment.

Table 7 Data for the UK air travel segment.

	1997	2000
No. employed in air transport	72 263	78 384
Travel expenditures (£bn)	17.9	21.8
No. of passengers carried (m)	146.7	179.9

Comment

As might be expected, there was continuing growth in all three measures in the late 1990s, as indeed there had been for many years prior to that. With regard to tourism, however, these trends were dramatically interrupted after the terror attacks on the USA on 11 September 2001.

Particular segment – Restaurants and hotels

Tables 8 and 9 show various data for restaurants and hotels in the UK.

Table 8 Data for UK restaurants

	1997	2001
Total sales (£m)	12 316	15 536
Of which:		
fast food (£m)	6 162	7 480
other restaurant and café meals (£m)	6 154	8 056
Total number of enterprises	43 200	46 790

Source: Restaurants 2002, KeyNote Ltd.

Table 9 Data for UK hotels by size of enterprise, 2000

Turnover (£000)	No. of enterprises
1–49	460
50–99	2005
100–249	3240
250–499	2035
500–999	1300
1000–4,999	1005
5000+	205
Total	10250

Comment

As might be expected, increased living standards have generated a growth in the turnover of restaurants in recent years, as well as in their number (Table 8). However, the number of hotels has actually fallen significantly, from 14410 in 1990 to the 10250 in 2000 shown in Table 9, which also shows the distribution of hotels by size of turnover in 2000.

Although no data are shown to demonstrate it, turnover of hotels grew much in line with that of restaurants during the 1990s, and the importance within that total of the larger establishments also increased.

Particular segment – Cinema, theatre etc.

Tables 10 and 11 show data for this segment of the UK leisure industry.

Table 10 Percentage of the GB population (aged 15 and over) who attended during the year

	1987/88	1993/94	1999/2000
Cinema	34	50	56
Theatre	24	24	23
Art galleries	21	22	22
Classical music	12	12	12
Ballet	6	7	6
Opera	5	7	6
Contemporary dance	4	3	4

Table 11 Data for cinemas, theatres and films

	1995	1999
No. of theatre admissions (m)	26	24
Theatre revenues (£m)	335	375
No. of cinema admissions (m)	115	139
Cinema revenues (£m)	353	556
No. of cinema screens	2,003	2,825
of which % at multiplex sites	38%	57%
Total expenditure on feature films (£m) (excludes video rental and purchase, and DVD)	1525	1893

Comment

Table 10 shows a remarkable consistency over time in audiences for different types of 'event', except for the dramatic growth in the proportion of the population attending cinemas. This in turn is reinforced in Table 11.

Particular segment – Libraries, museums etc.

Table 12 shows data for this segment of the UK leisure industry.

Table 12 Data for libraries, museums etc.

	1993–4	1998–9
Expenditure on museums and galleries (£m)	212	204
Expenditure on historic buildings and sites (£m)	164	144
Expenditure on public libraries	114	89
Public library lending (items issued, m)	582.1	495.2
of which audio–visual	31.6	37.9

Source: Department of Culture, Media & Sport; Loughborough University, 2000.

Comment

In contrast to virtually all previously included data, the trends here are clearly downward. Perhaps the spending cuts reflect overall government spending policy, or is it more a change in priorities? Are we reading less, or merely borrowing less from libraries?

Particular segment – Television and home entertainment

Table 13 shows data for television viewing in the UK. An OECD survey in 2000 showed 58.5 per cent of the UK population aged 16–65 watched more than two hours' of television per day, compared with 49.0 per cent in Germany, 39.5 per cent in the USA and only 21.5 per cent in Switzerland.

Table 13 Average UK weekly TV viewing, July 2000 (figures rounded)

	Average weekly viewing per person (h)		Share of total viewing (%)	
	All households	Households with satellite/ cable	All households	Households with satellite/ cable
Total BBC (BBC1, BBC2)	9.1	6.4	38.4	27.0
Total commercial (ITV, Ch4, Ch5)	10.6	7.7	44.9	32.8
Other	4.0	9.5	16.7	40.2
Totals	23.7	23.6	100	100

Source: Broadcasters' Audience Research Board (BARB), September 2000.

Table 14 shows data for home entertainment equipment in homes with children.

Table 14 Data for home entertainment equipment in homes with children (percentages)

	1993	1999
Video recorder	90	91
Teletext	53	80
CD player	33	65
Satellite TV dish	17	25
Video camera	17	23

Source: ITC, 2000.

Comment
Table 13 shows an interesting pattern of viewing between the three major TV broadcasting competitors, with the UK's tendency to watch TV more than other countries also highlighted. Table 14 shows the growth of home entertainment equipment over time, again no doubt a reflection of rising household incomes.

Particular segment – Professional sport (English soccer)
Figure 5 shows attendance figures at professional league football fixtures over nearly half a century.

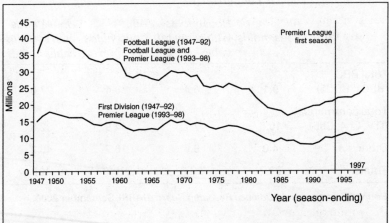

Figure 5 Professional league football attendances, 1947–1998

Source: S. Szymenski, Imperial College Management School

Comment
The long-term fall in attendances prior to the late 1980s is clear, presumably due to growing competition from other available leisure pursuits.

Conclusion and suggestions
The data contained in this chapter are merely illustrative. A huge volume of similarly relevant data is available, particularly on websites.

Correspondingly, any set of data can generate practice examination questions. The author's comments at the end of each section above are merely aimed to give a very brief summary of the main features. In virtually every case a question could be designed, perhaps with a standard format:

- to *summarize* the main features of the data
- to *explain* some economic relationship that is suggested by the data
- to *discuss* a possible issue or implication that the data might point towards.

Two examples are given below.

Based on Tables 4 and 6

1. Using Table 4, summarize the main trends in tourism to the UK in the period 1991–99.
2. Tourism is an aspect of international trade. Explain how the two-way flow of tourists shown in Table 6 between the UK and North America is consistent with the principle of comparative advantage.
3. Discuss the possible implications of the information in Tables 4 and 6 for the UK's balance of overseas payments.

Based on Tables 8 and 9, and the comment on them

1. Using Table 8, summarize the main trends in the UK restaurant sector in the period 1997–2001.
2. Whilst the number of restaurants has increased in recent years, the number of hotels has fallen, even though total turnover in both sectors has increased. One reason for this has been merger activity within the hotel sector. Explain possible economic reasons for such mergers.
3. Discuss possible implications for tourists to the UK of increasing concentration in the hotel sector.

Further reading

Atkinson, A., Units 9 and 23 in *Economics*, 3rd edn, Causeway Press, 2000.

Grant, S., Chapter 19 in *Stanlake's Introductory Economics*, 7th edn, Longman, 2000.

Gratton, C., and Taylor, P., *Economics of Sport and Recreation*, Spon Press, 2000.

Useful websites

Please visit www.heinemann.co.uk/hotlinks and enter the code 04545S.

Data response question

The following piece is adapted from *The Observer* of 13 January 2002. Read the article and then answer the questions.

High noon looms in battle for the high seas

War has broken out in the cruising industry – and to the victor will go leadership of one of the fastest-growing parts of the holiday market.

Battle commenced before Christmas, when Carnival, undisputed king of the market, launched a bid to sink the merger agreed between smaller rivals P&O Princess and Royal Caribbean the previous month.

So far, the fight has been restricted to verbal skirmishes but the battle is about to get serious. On 14 February, P&O's shareholders are due to vote on the merger, before which the onus is on Carnival to come up with a decent offer, without the pre-conditions and get-outs that hedged its initial approach.

Even the most hard-bitten gamblers would be reluctant to bet on the outcome. Carnival would certainly prefer the merger not to go ahead. RCP, as the merged company is provisionally known, would leapfrog Carnival to become the biggest operator, measured by number of berths. That is not a slot Carnival will give up lightly.

Carnival can take credit for creating the market in its current form. Its strategy of targeting ordinary Americans has fuelled the spectacular industry growth in the US – an average 8.4 per cent a year for the past two decades – and Europeans are now taking to the seas with equal enthusiasm.

Carnival has grown even more rapidly. Over the past decade, it increased its berths by an average of 11 per cent a year and now carries more than 2.6 million passengers a year. Earnings growth over the same period has averaged 15 per cent a year.

P&O Princess and Royal Caribbean have both been significant beneficiaries of the growth in the market. In 2001 alone they added five ships between them but both were still reporting bumper occupancy levels. At least until 11 September, that is. Like the rest of the travel industry, cruising suffered a big drop in demand in the wake of the terrorist attacks. P&O alone immediately lost around 20 000 bookings.

There are now signs of recovery, although only at the cost of big price cuts. Earlier this month, Carnival said bookings in the last weeks of 2001 were running 45 per cent ahead of the previous year but total bookings were still below last year's level. Occupancy levels for the first quarter are expected to be 92 per cent, compared with 99 per cent this time last year.

All three companies are confident this is just a temporary blip in the otherwise smooth progress of the cruising market.

They had better be right. P&O and Royal Caribbean have 14 ships, with 30 000 berths, on order over the next three years while Carnival is to take delivery of a further 14, offering more than 34 000 beds.

While some deliveries have been delayed after the terrorist attacks, for the industry as a whole there will still be 63 new ships on order over the next five years, increasing the number of beds available by 7 per cent a year.

One thing all three companies are agreed on is that the increases in capacity will quickly fill up. They may be right: only 12 per cent of Americans, and less than 2 per cent of Europeans, have been on a cruise but more than half would like to. It was those growth prospects, rather than thoughts of cutting costs or shedding jobs, that prompted P&O Princess and Royal Caribbean to get together.

When the deal was announced, the two companies pointed to the great geographic fit. As its name suggests, Royal Caribbean's strength is in the tropical islands while P&O operates more in the destination cruising market to places like Alaska. Royal Caribbean is relatively stronger in the US and P&O in Europe. A joint venture, agreed at the same time, was designed to address the relative weakness of both companies in southern Europe.

1. Identify *two* pieces of evidence given in the article, which support the claim that the cruising industry is 'one of the fastest-growing parts of the holiday market'. What further information would be needed to establish the truth or otherwise of this claim?   [5 marks]
2. Explain the statement 'In 2001 alone they added five ships between them but both were still reporting bumper occupancy levels'.

[3 marks]
3. Explain the main arguments used to justify the proposed merger between P&O Princess and Royal Caribbean.   [3 marks]
4. Explain why Carnival are likely to have wanted to prevent the proposed merger from happening.   [3 marks]
5. Given the long time period involved in generating new capacity in this industry ('63 new ships on order over the next five years'), discuss the problems involved in forecasting future demand.

[6 marks]

Chapter Five

Market structure of leisure industries

'Pleasure is the only thing worth having a theory about.'
Oscar Wilde, *The Picture of Dorian Gray*

Theory of market structures: characteristics and definitions

The ways in which firms behave, in particular in making decisions on price and output, are heavily influenced by the structure of the industries of which they are part. Economists traditionally identify four categories of **market structure**, the main characteristics of which are summarized in Table 16.

Table 16 The four principal market structures

Market structure	Number of firms	Products	Pricing	Entry
Perfect competition	Large	Homogeneous	Price-taker	Free
Absolute monopoly	One	One	Price-maker	Barriers
Monopolistic competition	Large	Differentiated	Price-maker	Free
Oligopoly	Few	Differentiated	Price-maker	Barriers

Both **perfect competition** and **absolute monopoly** are, in effect, extreme 'ideal types' of market structure, in the sense that they represent theoretical models, very rarely to be found in the real world (certainly no leisure industries come to mind which can be put in either category), but against which real industries can be compared.

Monopolistic competition and **oligopoly**, on the other hand, are very much the norm in the vast majority of industries, including the leisure sector.

What is the economist attempting to do in the study of market structures? Essentially, the first objective, having identified models with particular characteristics, is to analyse each market structure in terms of the way firms in it are likely to behave, and to draw conclusions concerning the consequences: for consumers, for the firms themselves, and for the overall working of the economy. These conclusions relate to price and output, to profitability, and to overall efficiency. Then, real world industries can be compared with the economists' models, their decision-making analysed and evaluated, and their behaviour forecast.

Of course, reality is almost always more complex than the theoretical models predict, so that analysis, evaluation and forecasting are rarely quite so straightforward as the previous paragraph might imply! However, it is as well to begin by making the aims clear. We shall now consider the named four market structures in detail.

Perfect competition

The essence of this theoretical extreme type of market structure is that, slightly strangely, there is no real competition in the everyday meaning of the word between the firms which make up the industry. This is because there are a large number of firms, all producing homogeneous (identical) products, and therefore each firm has no market power and so no freedom to set its own price. The price is determined through the interaction between market demand and supply forces. Each firm then accepts that price as a given, something outside its control, and is therefore a 'price-taker'. Further, firms outside the industry are free to enter it if they wish; there are no barriers preventing such entry (or, indeed, preventing the exit from the industry of existing firms).

Suppose that, in Figure 6(a), the market price is currently set at p_1. The firms in the industry are also assumed to operate with identical cost structures, represented by the AC and MC curves in Figures 6(a) and 6(c), since they are all assumed to have perfect knowledge of all factors affecting the industry. Then, each firm, with the objective of maximizing its total profit, will produce an output q_1, where the marginal cost of production is the same as the price.

This is because, if a firm produced an output below q_1, it would gain more profit by producing an extra unit, the extra revenue generated being greater than the extra cost incurred. Similarly, if current output were greater than q_1, profit would be increased by producing one fewer unit, the loss in revenue being less than the fall in costs.

Each firm, as shown in Figure 6(a), is earning a total **supernormal profit** represented by the shaded rectangular area, the supernormal profit per unit, cb (= da), multiplied by the number of units produced per period, ab (= dc).

However, this will be known to firms not currently operating in the industry. Since they are able to enter it freely, some will choose to do so, attracted by the prospect of themselves earning supernormal profit. This increase in industry supply, though – shown in Figure 6(b) as a shift to the right of the market supply curve – will cause market price to

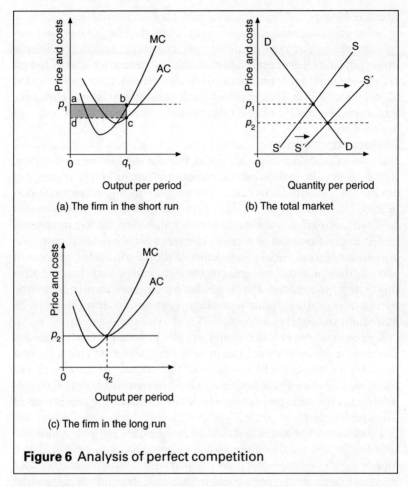

Figure 6 Analysis of perfect competition

(a) The firm in the short run

(b) The total market

(c) The firm in the long run

fall, so reducing both the profit-maximizing output of each firm, and the total profit it makes.

In the long run, the *equilibrium position* of the industry will occur when no outside firms can make **normal profit** if they enter, and no firms within the industry make below-normal profit, so that they have no desire to leave. This implies that all firms in the industry are in the position shown in Figure 6(c), with the whole market being in long-run equilibrium. Each firm produces q_2 output, and makes just normal profit, with market price at p_2.

Implications

It is worth observing at this stage that, in the above long-run equilibrium under conditions of perfect competition, each firm is producing at its least-cost level of output (q_2), and price is at its lowest possible level. There is **productive/technical efficiency**, in the sense that all production is at lowest possible cost, and there is also **allocative efficiency**, because price is also equal to the marginal cost of production.

Allocative efficiency, in terms of classical welfare economics, means that resources are optimally allocated, because the price of the product, which reflects how much value consumers put on the last unit of it purchased, is identical to how much it costs society to produce that unit.

When comparisons are made between different market structures, perfect competition can be seen to represent a form in which consumers are getting as good a deal as is possible. Within the industry, freedom of entry of new competitors guarantees that, in the long run, no firm makes any profit above what is needed for entrepreneurs to be willing to operate (normal profit), **average cost** of production is at its minimum, and so is price.

Within the overall economy, if all industries were perfectly competitive, resources would seem to be being allocated optimally, and the **invisible hand** of which Adam Smith famously wrote (*Wealth of Nations*, 1776) would be operating ideally to ensure that the society is solving its economic problem – of how best to allocate scarce resources – in a perfect manner.

This raises other issues, it should be stressed, for example relating to whether or not an allocation of scarce resources can ever be called 'optimal', when it depends on the unequal votes cast in the marketplace by consumers with very different incomes; but this is a broader question than is appropriate to discuss further in this context.

Absolute monopoly

This second extreme type of market structure can be regarded as being at the opposite end of the spectrum to perfect competition. It also demonstrates no real competition, but this time because the single firm which makes up the industry is protected from the entry of new firms by insurmountable barriers. These might be legal barriers – for example, the long-lasting prevention by the law in the UK of the delivery of letter post by anyone other than the Royal Mail – or they might be barriers created by the complete control of the absolute monopolist over a source of supply of a raw material used in the industry.

Whatever the reason for the entry barriers, the firm is in effect a complete price-maker. It cannot decide independently on both price and output, since it faces a demand curve, the product's market demand curve since the firm is the only one producing the product. However, it has freedom to choose price or output, in order to attempt to achieve whatever objectives it chooses to set for itself.

Under conditions of perfect competition, it is entirely sensible to assume that firms made decisions with the objective of maximizing profit. As was shown, in the long run, the maximum profit they can make is 'normal profit', the minimum needed to induce them to operate within the industry. (In the diagrams, since this normal profit is regarded by economists as a necessary cost of production, it is included as such in the cost curves.) This is not the case under conditions of absolute monopoly, however. Subject to the relationship between demand for the product and the cost conditions faced by the monopolist, it is likely that above-normal (supernormal) profit can be made. So the firm actually has a decision to make.

However, if we begin by continuing with the assumption of a profit-maximizing objective, the decision-making can be represented as in Figure 7.

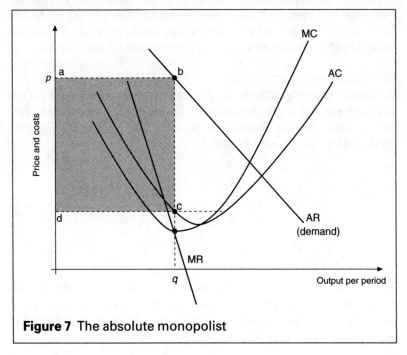

Figure 7 The absolute monopolist

Marginal revenue, the addition to the firm's total revenue which results from selling one extra unit of output, is now below the price (**average revenue**) being charged. This is because, given that the firm is sole seller of the product, so that the demand (AR) curve for its product is the downward-sloping market demand curve for the product as a whole, price has to be reduced in order to increase sales. This means that **marginal revenue** at any level of sales will be the price generated for the extra unit sold, less the loss of revenue caused by the price being lower than before on all other units sold.

Given the configuration shown in Figure 7 between cost and revenue curves, the same logic as was used for decision-making under conditions of perfect competition means that the profit-maximizing monopolist will choose to produce at output level q, where marginal revenue equates to **marginal cost**. Any change from this output would result in profit being reduced.

Given the demand curve, this then implies the decision to charge price p, in order to generate q sales. And this, in turn, means that the monopolist is making a total supernormal profit represented by the shaded area *abcd* per period.

The crucial attribute of absolute monopoly as a market structure, though, is the inability of new firms to enter the industry to compete with the monopolist. This means that this supernormal profit can continue to be generated into the long run, unlike in perfect (or, indeed, as will be shown in the next section, in monopolistic) competition.

Implications

It is clear that the differences in terms of outcome between perfect competition and absolute monopoly are stark. At least with the cost relationships shown, comparison between Figures 6(c) and 7 shows that, in the long run, with monopoly:

- the consumer is paying a higher price
- the firm is 'earning' supernormal profit
- less output is being produced
- production is not at the minimum average-cost, productively efficient, level
- production is not at the allocatively efficient level, since price is above marginal cost.

Too few resources are being allocated to the production of the product in question compared to the optimal position, because the monopolist is in effect creating artificial scarcity in order to push up price and so generate 'monopoly' profits.

Alternative scenarios

It is important to emphasize that the conclusions reached above are valid only given the assumptions made. Given the nature of monopoly, a number of somewhat different scenarios might well operate in reality, each of which would have implications for the outcomes generated.

Firstly, because it has no reason to fear competition, the monopolist may in fact produce less than perfectly efficiently, whatever the output. This is referred to as **X-inefficiency**, and implies AC and MC curves above those shown in Figure 7. The outcome would be even higher price and even lower output, a position still further away from the optimum from the consumers' or from society's point of view.

On the other hand, the monopolist may opt for price and output levels which generate *less* than maximum profit, so reducing the differences between the outcome generated and that which would result in perfect competition. This could be through genuine altruism – or it could be fear of government intervention, or some attempt at competition, if it were to make the very most of its profit potential.

It has so far been implicitly assumed that firms in both perfect competition and monopoly face identical U-shaped average cost curves (and corresponding marginal cost curves). The U-shape is the result of, first, overheads being spread over greater levels of output causing average cost to fall; and second beyond some level of output, variable cost per unit rising as **diminishing returns** set in, as the design capacity of the firm's fixed factors of production is approached. As this makes clear, the curves are essentially short run ones, the short run being defined as a period of time during which at least one factor of production, usually thought of as the size of the fixed capital, cannot be changed.

However, it may well be the case that, in the long run, the greater size of a firm with an absolute monopoly results in it being able to benefit from significant internal **economies of scale**; reductions in average cost resulting from greater scale of production. Furthermore, one school of thought also argues that, through being able to earn supernormal profit, monopolists will use some of such surpluses to research and to innovate, thereby maybe improving the quality of products available, and/or reducing production costs.

In these cases, static comparisons between the two extreme market structures are no longer valid. The advantages which result from the nature of a perfectly competitive structure may, or may not, be outweighed by the lower costs of absolute monopoly in such circumstances.

Monopolistic competition

This market structure is very closely approximated in many industries, including leisure industries, in the real world. It involves a large number of firms, with freedom of entry into, and exit from, the industry. However, unlike in perfect competition, each firm produces a good or service which is differentiated to a greater or lesser extent from those produced by its competitors. So each firm also has at least some freedom to set its own price.

The analysis of the behaviour of firms in such a market structure is along familiar lines, and can be summarized as in Figures 8(a) and (b).

Again assuming profit maximization – as will be seen below, this is again a sensible assumption here – and with the same cost curves as previously, in the short run price and output will be at p and q respectively in Figure 8(a).

Each firm faces a downward-sloping demand curve for its product, probably reflecting much greater price elasticity of demand than for the absolute monopolist, given the extent of substitutability which exists in consumers' eyes between the products of the different firms in the industry. Each firm will achieve maximum profit at the output at which MC = MR. Indeed, it will be seen that Figure 8(b) is similar to Figure 7 because, in the short run, analysis of the firm in monopolistic competition is close to that for the absolute monopolist. The difference lies in the more elastic demand (and so flatter AR and MR curves) facing the firm in monopolistic competition.

However, the attraction to firms outside the industry of supernormal profits being made within it will ensure that, in the long run, given that it is possible this time, new firms will enter the industry. The result is a reduction in the demand for the products being sold by existing firms; a shift to the left of their AR (and MR) curve, with a corresponding reduction of their profit-maximizing output, and of their profits.

This process will continue until new firms can no longer make normal profit by entering the industry, with no existing firm generating below normal profit. At this point, the industry can be thought of as being in equilibrium; the 'marginal firm' – for whom staying in the industry is just worthwhile – will be making maximum profit (like all others, where MC = MR), which is only normal profit (thus, price, AR = AC). Figure 8(b) shows the position of this firm in long-run equilibrium: price will be p_1 and output q_1.

Implications

Let us again compare outcomes. As Figure 8(b) illustrates, as in perfect competition, the ability of new firms to enter the industry ensures that

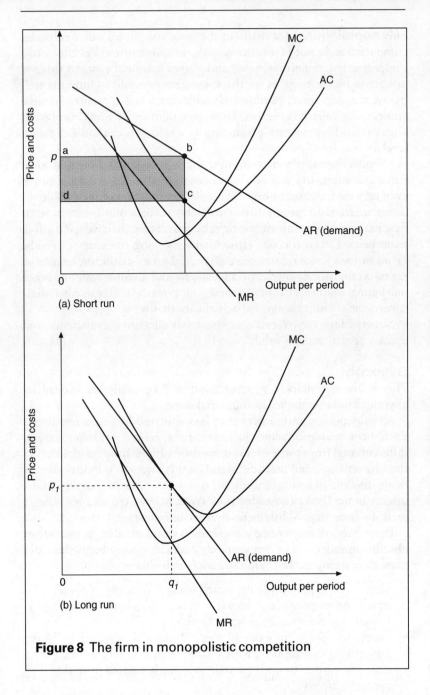

Figure 8 The firm in monopolistic competition

only normal profits are made in the long run. In all other respects, comparisons do not favour monopolistic competition. Price is above the perfectly competitive level, and above marginal cost, so there is allocative inefficiency, as for the absolute monopolist. Output is well below the optimum, productively efficient level; the entry of new competition here has resulted in a large number of firms competing with each other, but each producing well below its optimum capacity level.

It is possible under conditions of monopolistic competition that some firms in the industry will be able to generate some supernormal profit even into the long run, in fact. This will be a function of their ability to *differentiate* their product (or products) successfully from those of existing and new competitors, thereby preventing their demand curve from being forced too far leftwards by the long-run entry of rivals. Firms in such a market structure do indeed go to significant lengths to try to do this, for example, by advertising and a whole range of other marketing methods (though these, of course, will eat into their supernormal profit earning capacity in another way).

Nevertheless, the overall conclusions of allocative inefficiency and excess capacity remain valid.

Oligopoly

This is another market structure that will be easily recognized by anyone familiar with the UK industrial scene.

An oligopoly is an industry that is dominated by just a few firms. Each firm sells products which are, to a greater or lesser extent, differentiated from those of its competitors. Firms have freedom to set their own prices, and there are significant barriers to the entry of new firms into the industry (and often, too, to the exit of existing firms, usually in the form of so-called **sunk costs**, heavy expenditures already made by firms to establish themselves in the industry).

These barriers may not be completely insurmountable, as they are in absolute monopoly, but they certainly make new entry very difficult in most circumstances. They are commonly in the form of:

- sizeable economies of scale, which make it virtually impossible for new firms to produce at an average cost anywhere near as low as those being achieved by existing firms
- consumer loyalty to existing firms' brands, buttressed by heavy advertising expenditure, which means that it is very difficult for a new competitor to grab enough of a market share to enable it to compete effectively.

The crucial aspect of oligopoly, which makes analysis of decision-making within it rather different from that in the previously discussed three types of market structure, is that the firms are not independent of each other in their decision-making. Because there are only a small number of firms within the industry, it would be idle to assume that each made decisions about price and output, for example, without taking some cognizance of the likely response of competitors.

This interdependence implies that it is not possible to develop a simple model of the behaviour of each firm, because each firm's decision-making depends on that of other firms, or on how it assumes other firms would react to its own decisions.

What, then, can the economist contribute to an explanation of how oligopolistic firms behave? Beyond the initial conclusion that there is no single, unique set of prices and outputs which can be said to engender achievement of, say, profit-maximizing equilibrium positions for each firm, given interdependence, the implications of the characteristics of oligopoly can be considered under a number of subheadings.

Collusion

One way in which firms could operate would be, in effect, to cooperate with each other so as to act as though they formed a single monopolist. Thus, total industry output would be that which equated marginal revenue with marginal cost, with a corresponding relatively high level of market price, and total supernormal profit equivalent to what would be available if there were an absolute monopoly.

Agreement – or **collusion** – between the firms would be needed so that this outcome was reached, and there would also have to be agreement about the way sales (and profits) were shared out between the firms which made up the oligopoly. Such collusion could in principle be 'open' (formally organized and publicly acknowledged to exist) or it could be more hidden, or tacit.

For a number of reasons, however, it is unlikely that such an extreme position would exist or persist. For one thing, governments tend to legislate against anti-competitive behaviour, on the grounds that it is against the public interest.

Also, from the point of view of an individual firm, there is a conflict between behaving in an agreed way so as to play its part in maximizing profit for the whole industry, and making decisions which could increase its own profits. This conflict itself is likely to prevent the theoretical absolute monopoly solution from being the outcome in oligopoly for any length of time.

- When market demand falls, for example, it is very likely that at least some individual firms will choose to break the agreement to try to sustain their own profitability, even if it is at the expense of that of other firms.
- When technology changes, or new markets or new products are developed, again it is likely that some firms will feel the need to try to gain disproportionately from the opportunities available.
- Furthermore, although entry of new firms may be difficult, it is not impossible; and if existing firms are operating cosily to make large supernormal profits, the chances of new competition are inevitably greater.

Price stability
The interdependence which exists between firms in oligopoly means that there is likely to be asymmetry in the response of demand for a firm's product to a price change, depending on whether price is raised or lowered.

- If price is raised, the quantity demanded might be expected to fall quite significantly, as the firm loses customers to its rivals, who see no need to raise their prices in response (though see the discussion of price leadership below).
- If price is cut, not much extra demand might be generated, because rival firms are quite likely also to cut prices, in an attempt to retain their own shares of the market.

The result is that, whatever the current level of prices, profitability would fall if they are changed in either direction; hence the tendency for prices to remain fairly stable, relative to each other, amongst firms in an oligopoly.

Price leadership
From time to time, of course, prices do change in oligopolistic industries, and often this is achieved through **price leadership**.

Most commonly, this happens because of changes in costs of production, which are experienced by all the firms in the industry, though there can be other circumstances too; for example, changes in total market demand, or the perceived threat of significant new competition.

It is, perhaps, most easily observed in the UK amongst petrol retailers; one firm increases price by 3p per litre, say, and within days the same change is made by all the other firms.

In some industries one firm may be dominant, and its price leadership is regularly followed by other firms in the industry. In others, though, the role of price leader merely rotates between different firms, none of whom has a dominant market share, but all of whom share an interest in the price change.

Price wars and non-price competition

The innate conflict that exists for firms in oligopoly has already been referred to, between behaviour that is in the interest of the profitability of all, and behaviour that is in the interest of the profitability of one at the expense of that of others.

This is most clearly evident in pricing decisions. Sometimes, for example, unsuccessful examples of price leadership can be observed. One oligopolist increases or reduces price, the others do not follow, and the first quite soon reverts to its original position. Essentially, the reason is likely to relate to the fear which firms have in this market structure of becoming involved in a **price war**.

The reason for such a fear is entirely rational. If firms engaging in competitive price-cutting with the objective of increasing market share – and thereby profitability – have roughly equal power, the outcome is most likely to be good news for consumers, but merely lower profits for all firms, with little change in market shares.

The logical response, of course, is exactly what is generally observed in oligopolistic industries; that competition amongst the firms takes a wide variety of non-price forms, such as advertising, special offers, new product development, cost-reducing innovations. These are all aimed at increasing the profitability of the firms which engage in them, but without the fear of the possibly catastrophic effects of direct price competition.

Occasionally, however, a price war does break out, for example, though perhaps to a more limited extent than is sometimes realized or claimed, between the large UK supermarkets. There are two likely scenarios.

- One is when one firm in the oligopoly is performing poorly, and in effect initiates a price war out of desperation.
- A more likely scenario is when a firm believes itself to be the likely winner. It initiates the price war from a position of strength, perhaps reflecting a greater asset base, for example, and believes it will be able to survive the period of reduced profits for all more effectively than its rivals. It may be correct, of course; but it is clearly a strategy not without risk.

Non-profit-maximizing objectives

The assumption that firms have the objective of maximizing profit is entirely sensible for the models of perfect and monopolistic competition. This is not the case, however, when competition is between firms in an oligopoly, if for no other reason than that inter-dependence means that there is no unique profit-maximizing output/price decision to be identified.

Much empirical study of firms' decision-making has emphasized that there are a range of objectives – short-term survival, long-term growth, maximum share price, profit 'satisficing', the chief executive's social status, for example – which influence the way in which different firms make decisions at different times.

In private sector enterprises profit will always be a significant objective. Given the nature of oligopoly, however, it is likely that other objectives will also play a part for firms in this type of market structure.

Market structures in leisure industries

When one is analysing a particular leisure industry, to what extent is the above economic analysis helpful? Do the economists' characterizations of the nature of the four market structures, and the consequent behaviour of firms within them, make it easier to understand, to explain and perhaps also to predict the way in which particular leisure industries operate, and the decision-making of individual firms within them? One would hope so; if not, there would be very large question marks as to whether the theory has any merit at all!

Of the four market structures, perfect competition and absolute monopoly are extreme cases, which probably do not exist in practice in any leisure industry. The requirements of product homogeneity and price-takers probably rule out the practical applicability of perfect competition in this sector, and likewise absolute monopoly, because of the requirement that **barriers to entry** are complete. These theoretical market structures are there largely as *benchmarks*, against which particular industries can be compared in terms of their prices, their output, and their productive and allocative efficiency.

In practice, then, we would expect the models of monopolistic competition and oligopoly to provide the aids in reality to the understanding being sought. Thus, when considering any particular leisure industry, a number of questions should be asked.

- Is the industry dominated by a few firms, or are there quite a large number of relatively small firms?

- How similar are the products produced by different firms, or is there significant differentiation between them in the eyes of consumers?
- How much freedom do competing firms have in practice to set their own prices?
- How easy or how difficult is it, in practice or at least in principle, for firms outside the industry to become effective competitors within it? How easy is it, similarly, for existing firms to choose to abandon the industry? (These questions relate to the extent to which the industry is or is not genuinely 'contestable'.) What barriers to entry in fact exist?
- How profitable is the industry? This should relate both to individual firms within it, and to the industry as a whole *vis-à-vis* other industries.
- Do significant economies of scale exist, and if so how big are the cost advantages they yield to larger firms?
- How productively efficient are the firms? Is there evidence of X-inefficiency? Is there significant excess capacity?
- To what extent is there collusion between firms in the industry?

Answering questions such as these – and the list is not meant to be exhaustive – should enable the analyst to draw valuable conclusions.

You will probably already have made cross-connections between the previous paragraph and some of the leisure industries identified in Chapters 2 and 4. It is not the objective here to give a detailed analysis of each leisure industry in the UK, but rather to provide a toolbox which you can use to help you undertake such analysis. It is worth concluding by referring to a few examples.

Air travel
Air travel has for many years been a good example of oligopoly in practice. Economies of scale in operation are very significant, and these, as well as heavy regulation, have acted as major barriers to entry. There are huge sunk costs too.

However, the dramatic growth of so-called 'low cost' carriers has had a major impact on the structure of the industry in recent years, demonstrating that barriers to entry are not always as significant, over time, as they may appear.

Reduction in worldwide demand for air travel resulting from external shocks is also having important consequences for the structure, and profitability, of the industry. It would not be at all surprising, either, if growing concern over the environmental impact of air travel were to have similar consequences in the future.

Television

TV broadcasting is another UK leisure industry which has traditionally been heavily oligopolistic, with important barriers to entry. However, this is another sector which has seen considerable developments in recent years – satellite and digital TV in particular – which have resulted in much greater **contestability**.

There is also an ongoing debate about the extent and forms of state regulation which is appropriate in the sector. The outcome of this will also have serious consequences for the structure, working and profitability of the industry.

An additional complication, which raises the issue of the objectives of firms in a novel way, is the 'public service broadcasting' function of the BBC, as well as the contrast between its reliance for revenue on the licence fee and that of other 'competitors' on advertising revenues, subscriptions, pay-per-view, etc.

Spectator sports

The spectator sports 'industry' also raises the question of profitability versus other objectives to an important extent. Indeed, study of the industry – or is it more a series of non-competing sub-industries? – probably raises rather more interesting questions than it answers.

There is an obvious element of freedom of entry in individual spectator sports such as tennis or golf (though perhaps increasingly less so in top soccer); but how much effective freedom of entry is there for new sports in the totality of the spectator sports market?

The relative lack of success in recent years of American football, basketball and women's golf might argue the case that barriers are very strong. But some success in ice hockey and club rugby union in some local areas might put a counter-argument.

How important is profit as compared with playing successes in the hierarchy of objectives of top Premiership soccer clubs? If one or a small number of clubs monopolize playing success, could this reduce demand for the overall 'product'?

How important is the generation of revenue directly from spectators, in the long run as well as the short run, compared with that obtained from other sources such as TV and sponsorship?

Package holidays

The package holiday market/industry is much more orthodox in terms of use of the theory of market structures as an aid to analysing it. In the UK, although it can be argued that it is dominated by only three or four large operators, so that one would expect oligopolistic-type behaviour and profitability, there are also important extents to which it is contestable. Outside firms are genuinely able, at least in more specialist niches, to enter as effective competitors.

The outcomes can then be analysed in terms of the models: development of new markets; integration to try to reduce costs; occasional price wars; heavy attempts to differentiate products.

KEY WORDS

Market structure	Marginal revenue
Perfect competition	Marginal cost
Absolute monopoly	X-inefficiency
Monopolistic competition	Diminishing returns
Oligopoly	Economies of scale
Supernormal profit	Sunk costs
Normal profit	Collusion
Productive/technical efficiency	Price leadership
Allocative efficiency	Price war
Average cost	Barriers to entry
Invisible hand	Contestability
Average revenue	

Further reading

Atkinson, A., Unit 55 in *Economics*, 3rd edn, Causeway Press, 2000.

Bamford, C., and Munday, S., Chapter 7 in *Markets*, Heinemann Educational, 2002.

Griffiths, A., and Ison, S., Chapters 3–7 in *Business Economics*, Heinemann Educational, 2001.

Essay topics

1. TV broadcasting used to be regarded as a clear example of an oligopoly, but recent developments in broadcasting technology have made the market very much more contestable.

   (a) Explain the behaviour of firms in an oligopolistic market.

   [10 marks]

   (b) Discuss the likely implications for firms and consumers of the recent developments in broadcasting technology. [15 marks]

   [OCR 2002]

2. The existence of many small high street travel agents, each working well below capacity, is a sign of inefficiency.

(a) Using diagrams, explain the short- and long-run equilibrium positions of a firm in monopolistic competition. [10 marks]

(b) Discuss the view that greater efficiency would result if the travel agent industry showed more characteristics of monopoly.

[15 marks]

[OCR 2002]

Useful website

- *Financial Times*: please go to www.heinemann.co.uk/hotlinks and enter code 04545S.

Data response question

Read the piece 'Travel firms venture into cyberspace', which is adapted from *Mail on Sunday* of 3 March 2002. Then answer the questions.

Travel firms venture into cyberspace

Holidaymakers will soon be able to book online with all four of the major tour operators. Thomas Cook was the first to offer Internet booking in April 1999. MyTravel, formerly called Airtours, and Thomson Travel have followed suit in the past three months, and First Choice says its online booking will be up and running this month.

More than half of all holidays taken each year by Britons are booked with one of the big four, which specialize in selling flight and accommodation packages. These inclusive breaks are the mainstay of high street travel agents, which could suffer further falls in business if online booking takes off.

Internet holiday bookings account for a tiny proportion of the total so far, but reservations made through travel agents have fallen from 70 per cent to 55 per cent in the past ten years.

Consumer researcher Mintel says the people most likely to reserve online are those who travel more independently, buying flights and accommodation separately.

Thomas Cook says that, so far, its online booking service has been mostly used by new customers to book flights only or city breaks.

Table A Data for the travel industry

	Domestic holidays		Holidays abroad	
	Millions of holidays	Money spent (£bn)*	Millions of holidays	Money spent (£bn)**
1996	64.8	10.7	26.8	12.1
1997	70.8	11.9	29.1	12.7
1998	68.8	11.2	32.2	14.3
1999	71.0	12.7	35.0	16.6
2000	68.0	12.7	36.7	18.0
2001***	63.0	12.3	37.8	18.0

*Pound sterling at 2001 value. ** Excluding fares to and from the UK. ***Estimate.

Figure A Passengers booked with the big air travel groups by June 2001 (thousands)

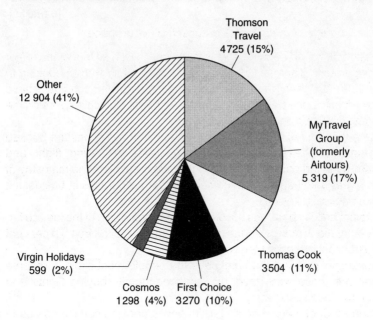

1. Using Table A:
   (a) Compare the trends in the number of holidays taken by Britons domestically and abroad in the period 1996 to 2001.   [3 marks]
   (b) What conclusions can be drawn about expenditure per holiday domestically and overseas?   [3 marks]
2. Using Figure A:
   (a) What market structure best describes the holiday air travel market? Justify your answer.   [2 marks]
   (b) Explain, in the light of your answer to (a), how you would expect the firms involved to compete with each other.   [6 marks]
3. During the past ten years, Britons have been taking more holidays per year, booking them earlier, and booking more of them independently, rather than through travel agents or through tour operators directly. Given these trends, and given the likelihood of further growth in Internet booking, discuss the possible implications for consumers and for the profits of the holiday firms.
   [6 marks]

Chapter Six

Leisure and the national economy

'Increased means and increased leisure are the two civilizers of man.'
Benjamin Disraeli, Manchester speech, 3 April 1872

The impact of leisure industries

Data have already been presented in Chapter 4 demonstrating the importance of the leisure sector within the UK economy. Furthermore, the full importance is considerably greater than these figures suggest, for two reasons.

- In particular areas and regions, the leisure sector is the major employer; for example, tourism in Devon and Cornwall. Where this is the case, the health, and growth over time, of the sector is clearly of huge importance to the whole economy of the region/area involved.
- The impact of leisure industries is measured not only by their direct share in GDP or employment. They also generate demand for a whole range of ancillary goods and services. Tourism, for example, creates an important market for local agricultural produce and for local manufacturers in areas where it predominates. Fuel is consumed in vast quantities as a result of air travel and indeed all forms of transport linked to leisure markets. Spectator sports, and also participation in sporting activities, generates demand for associated merchandise, from soccer replica shirts to tennis racquets.

If we take elementary analysis of the working of the macro economy to be in terms of the interplay between **aggregate demand** (AD) and **aggregate supply** (AS), it is clear that the output of UK leisure industries is a significant contributor to AS, and that the demand for their products is an important element in AD, both directly and indirectly. Thus, any change in demand for the products of the leisure industries, or in their output, will have consequences at the national level for the four most commonly identified macroeconomic policy variables: total employment and unemployment levels; the rate of inflation; the rate of economic growth; and the balance of overseas payments. It will also have consequences for the particular leisure sectors directly affected. Two recent UK examples will perhaps help to illustrate.

Example 1

The terrorist attacks on the World Trade Center in New York in September 2001 had, as one of their consequences, an increase in the perceived risk of air travel, amongst consumers and potential consumers. Thus, there was a significant fall in the demand for tourism worldwide. There has been a major microeconomic impact on the airline industry, of course, but also a significant deflationary macroeconomic effect in a number of countries. Reduced AD consequent upon the fall in demand for tourism would be forecast by the economist to result in higher unemployment, lower inflation, lower growth and reduced imports.

Example 2

The holding of the Commonwealth Games in Manchester in the summer of 2002 had different, and more beneficial, macroeconomic consequences. Investment in facilities required to hold the Games increased the supply-potential not just of the parts of the North West directly involved, but of the UK as a whole. The extra demand generated caused national output and employment to be greater than they would otherwise have been.

Artistic industries

The UK's artistic industries accounted for 5% of gross domestic product in 2002. They generated £127bn revenue, exports of £12bn and employed approximately 1.3m people. These industries include design, film, music, publishing, software and computers, TV and music. Recent years have witnessed a significant growth in the output of, and employment in, the computers, film and television industries. The UK is also seen as a world leader in design and has the world's third biggest recorded music market.

Government macroeconomic policy and the leisure sector

The relationship between the leisure sector and the macro economy is not just one way, of course. Just as changes in demand and/or supply in the leisure sector have macroeconomic consequences, so also changes in the macroeconomy impact upon leisure industries. In particular, when a government changes its macroeconomic policy weapons, in order to attempt to achieve some policy objective(s), leisure industries are affected no less, and sometimes more, than others.

Interest rates

The UK government has now delegated short-term control of **interest rates** to the Monetary Policy Committee of the Bank of England, which is charged with maintaining a given inflation rate target. When such interest rate changes occur, they impact upon all sectors of the UK economy, including the leisure sector. Thus, for example, if the rate of interest is increased, there would be:

- a tendency for firms to cancel, or at least postpone, planned investment, for example in new plant, because of the increased cost of borrowing to finance the investment, or because the expected rate of return on the investment is no longer above the cost of financing it
- increased interest costs for all firms with significant debt, either in the form of overdrafts, or longer-term finance
- reduced demand, because of the effect on consumers' spending of the higher interest rates.

Reduced demand is likely to be of particular importance for firms in the leisure sector, since often spending on their products is the first to be reduced when disposable incomes fall.

Fiscal policy

An alternative (or complementary) policy for governments aiming to achieve macroeconomic objectives is **fiscal policy**; changes in direct and/or indirect taxation, and/or in the government's own expenditure on goods and services.

Spending on leisure products tends to be regarded as very much in the 'luxuries' category by most consumers, and so tends to be particularly heavily hit when income taxes are increased. Similarly, a rise in indirect taxes, or a cut in government expenditure, reduces disposable incomes, and so leisure spending falls disproportionately.

Of course, if either interest rate or fiscal policy changes are in the opposite direction, so that they have expansionary macroeconomic effects, leisure industries, by the same logic, tend to benefit disproportionately too. This has important consequences for the industries. To be successful in the long run they need to be as flexible as possible; able to increase capacity and output quickly when the economy is in an upswing, but also able to cope with sizeable falls in demand when the need arises. This is by no means easy to achieve, but flexible employment policies, as low as possible fixed costs, and minimum possible reliance on long-term debt, would all be ideal recipes.

Exchange rates

Exchange rates change for a variety of reasons, including sometimes government intervention, and can have important consequences for some leisure sectors.

Tourism is probably affected more than most, given how important overseas demand is for the tourist industry in the UK. If we take, for example, a fall in the value of the pound sterling (whether inside or outside the eurozone) against the US dollar, the demand for tourism in the UK amongst US citizens will rise; the more so, the greater is the relevant price elasticity of demand. This is because the US dollar will buy more pounds sterling than previously, so that the UK becomes a more attractive destination for US tourists.

The disadvantage to UK firms of a reduced external value of the pound is that costs of imports into the UK increase, but this is usually a much smaller effect than the beneficial one on demand.

The leisure sector and the environment

The growth in spending on leisure activities represents an increase in living standards of the population. Furthermore, the increase in leisure time at the expense of time at work – whether measured by reduced hours worked per week, or by reduced years spent working relative to time spent in retirement – indubitably represents an increase in quality of life even if it is not reflected in **real GDP per head**.

It is worth noting that growing concerns about the 'demographic time bomb', with the proportion of elderly forecast to grow significantly in the decades ahead relative to those of working age, seems likely to result in reduced years of retirement in the future.

It should also be pointed out that some leisure sectors also have harmful consequences for the quality of life, in that they generate **negative externalities**: disadvantageous consequencies for third parties not directly involved in an economic transaction. One glaring example concerns air travel, which generates huge volumes of environmental pollution. The impact of tourism on environmentally sensitive areas is another; the more tourists visit areas of natural beauty, or areas inhabited by rare wildlife, the more damage is caused, and the less attractive and extensive will such areas be to others in the future. The growth of 'eco-tourism' is one reflection of growing public awareness in this context.

Whenever negative externalities are generated, economic analysis suggests that government intervention in one form or another may well be appropriate. Although it is beyond the scope of this book to consider such possible action in detail, it would be wrong to ignore the fact that growing leisure time and leisure pursuits create problems as well as generating huge benefits.

The box below discusses some of the benefits and costs that the tourism industry can generate for an economy.

The effects of tourism

Income and employment

The growth of the tourist industry has increased income and employment in a number of countries. This effect can be greater than it first appears. Obviously, tourists create income and employment directly for the hotels, restaurants and attractions which cater for tourists. But they also create income and employment in a wide range of other industries. Some of these are ones which supply goods and services to the tourist industry such as insurance firms, farms and taxi firms. Others are ones which benefit from spending by local people and firms arising from the income brought in by the tourists. So an initial rise in income of, say, £30 million in an area and the creation of 2000 extra jobs may eventually lead to a rise in income of £90 million and 5000 more jobs. This knock-on effect on income and employment is referred to as the **tourism income multiplier.**

However, the initial jobs created in the tourist industry may not be of a very high quality as many are unskilled. Workers in the tourist industry also tend not to be very well paid. In addition, the effect on income and employment will not be very great if a significant proportion of the goods and services used in the tourist industry are bought in from abroad. For example, a hotel in Petra in Jordan run by a UK company may buy some of its furniture and linen from the UK. Some of the senior staff it employs may also come from the UK.

The balance of payments

The effects on the country's balance of payments position will also be influenced by where the firms in the tourist industry obtain their materials and food from and the national origin of the firms. The UK firm running the hotel in Petra will send profits back to the UK.

Countries not only have tourists visiting them but also their own citizens are tourists in other countries, so in the trade in service section of the balance of payments there is both a credit and debit item.

Culture

Where there are notable differences in the income levels and culture of the tourists and the local inhabitants social tensions may arise. Tourists may act in a way, for example, getting drunk and gambling, which upsets the sensibility of the locals, and their greater spending power may result in resources being switched from meeting the needs of locals to meeting the needs of the tourists. For example, houses for locals may be demolished in order to build hotels.

Local culture may be threatened by the presence of tourists in a number of ways. One is referred to as the **demonstration effect.** This is where the locals, particularly the younger locals, copy the culture of the tourists, especially in terms of clothes, films, music, food, drink and social attitudes. The presence of tourists, especially wealthy ones, changes the types of goods and services demanded and thereby changes the skills and working patterns of the locals. The process whereby contact with tourists actually changes the culture of a country is called **acculturation.**

Environment

Tourism may damage the environment in a number of ways including:

- visual pollution; the building of hotels, funfairs, etc. can reduce the visual attractiveness of an area
- noise and air pollution caused by, for example, the planes and coaches transporting the tourists

- waste generated by the tourists
- congestion arising from the influx of tourists and people catering for the needs of tourists
- destruction of the natural environment, for example, to build golf courses and ski slopes for tourists
- heavy use of water supplies, often in areas where the locals are short of water.

The ability of an area to cope with tourists in a way that does not damage the features that attract the tourists in the first place is referred to as its **carrying capacity.**

Source: Economics in Context, by S. Grant and C. Vidler, Heinemann Educational, 2000.

KEY WORDS

Aggregate demand	Negative externalities
Aggregate supply	Tourism income multiplier
Interest rates	Demonstration effect
Fiscal policy	Acculturation
Exchange rates	Carrying capacity
Real GDP per head	

Further reading

Grant, S., Chapter 7 in *Economic Growth and Business Cycles*, Heinemann Educational, 1999.

Grant, S., and Vidler, C., Part 2 unit 11 in *Economics in Context*, Heinemann Educational, 2000.

Tribe, J., *The Economics of Leisure and Tourism*, 2nd edn, Butterworth–Heinemann, 1999.

Useful website

- Office for National Statistics: please go to www.heinemann. co.uk/hotlinks and enter code 04545S.

Essay topics

1. Real GNP per head is the usual measure used to compare living standards over time. Discuss the impact on living standards of:

(a) a 10 per cent reduction in hours worked by all full-time employees

(b) a decision to impose a charge on all who hike in national parks, to reflect the environmental damage they cause.   [25]

2. Discuss the possible impact on a top UK professional soccer club of:

   (a) a rise in the standard rate of income tax

   (b) a fall in the exchange rate of the pound sterling

   (c) a rise in the rate of interest.   [25]

Data response question

Read the piece 'Britain's great big gamble', which is adapted from *The Observer* of 24 March 2002. Then answer the questions.

Britain's great big gamble

Britain is set for a gambling binge. On Tuesday the government will announce plans to liberalize and deregulate the gaming sector in what will be the most far-reaching reform seen for 40 years.

Tight restrictions imposed on casinos, bookmakers and bingo in the 1960s will be scrapped.

Among the changes outlined will be provision for more casinos with more slot machines – and these machines will be linked, thereby offering tantalizing million-pound jackpots. The jackpot limit now is just £1000.

Delighted casino operators will be allowed to advertise. The 24-hour rule, which forces new punters to wait a day before they can enter a casino, will be axed. Further consultation on whether punters can drink at the gaming tables is expected, but live entertainment Vegas-style will be waved through.

Top bingo prizes will double to a million pounds. More betting shops will open as the restrictive demand criteria are lifted. And they, too, will be able to house more slot machines, again offering bigger prize money, though not on the scale of casinos.

Tuesday's announcement will usher in casino clusters in places like Blackpool, Southend and Margate.

Those in favour of the changes argue that high-quality gaming centres, equipped with hotels and conference facilities, will boost British tourism and allow the regeneration of down-at-heel British coastal resorts.

But while the government wants to please as many sub-sectors of the leisure industry as possible, the pub industry's bid to host betting games will be rejected.

There will be other serious casualties. Liberalization will double the losses UK punters incur from gambling. The tell-tale 'stake less win' figures, including the National Lottery, will rise from their current £7.5 billion to £15 billion once all the measures are adopted, according to research from Peter Collins, the UK's leading gaming academic, based at the University of Salford.

But the City will be delighted. Liberalization will trigger flotations or trade sales that may well involve all seven of Britain's leading gambling businesses being buoyed by the prospect of fat new revenue streams.

Proposals to allow a mix of soft gaming (such as bingo), and hard betting (casino games and slot machines) under one roof, which will be permitted next week, have divided the industry. Some say it is not clear whether the higher tax yield from more betting for the Treasury will offset the cost of coping with problem gambling.

Sir Peter Fry, head of the Bingo Association, fears many small bingo operators will go out of business as a result of the soft–hard mix: 'I believe clearing up the effects of problem gambling will cost more money than the Treasury will accrue.' His comments have, not surprisingly, been strongly rejected by the rest of the industry.

Betting firms will have to contribute more to organizations that tackle problem gambling and will be forced to be socially responsible.

The liberalization is the final piece in a jigsaw that has seen the gaming sector emerge as a City favourite over the past two years. Last year the government abolished betting tax, which saw 9 per cent of stake money go to the Treasury. Now, the government taxes firms' gross profits at 15 per cent. The result has seen bookies' turnover rise by 40 per cent.

The prospect of more slot machines is especially welcomed by the industry. 'Machines don't go sick, or demand overtime,' said one industry leader. In other words, they are a cash cow and potentially addictive – as the authorities in Australia have found. There, liberalization created huge social problems and the Canberra government is now attempting to backtrack on reform. The prospect of slot halls will fill many backbench MPs and religious leaders with horror.

1. Identify *two* benefits argued by those in favour of the anticipated deregulation of the UK gaming industry. [2 marks]
2. Britain's 'Big Seven' leading gambling businesses, in alphabetical order, are Coral Eurobet, Gala, Ladbrokes, LCI, Rank, Stanley Leisure and William Hill. Mergers between them are forecast.
   (a) What are the essential characteristics of an oligopoly? [3 marks]
   (b) Explain the likely consequences for 'consumers' of:
   (i) the anticipated deregulation of the gaming industry [4 marks]
   (ii) future mergers between firms in the industry. [4 marks]

3. Discuss Sir Peter Fry's view: 'I believe cleaning up the effects of problem gambling will cost more money than the Treasury will accrue'. [7 marks]

Chapter Seven

Further data response questions

'To be able to fill leisure intelligently is the last product of civilization.
Bertrand Russell, *The Conquest of Happiness*

This chapter offers a broad range of data response questions. The intention is to provide you with more information about the leisure sector, and many additional opportunities to apply your knowledge of economic concepts in the analysis and evaluation of key issues in the sector. We start, appropriately, with 'Game on'. Enjoy!

Q1 – Television and the Premiership League

The following piece is reproduced from *The Guardian* of 7 October 2002.

Game on

It seems fitting for a game so driven by passion that English football's flagship league, the Premiership, owes its livelihood to a week when 'the world went mad'. That is how Greg Dyke, the BBC's director-general, described the bidding frenzy in June 2000, when BskyB, ITV and NTL bid a total of £1.6 billion for television rights to the league and broadcasters appeared to throw caution, and business sense, to the wind.

Some say the biggest problem facing Premier League chief executive Richard Scudamore is the fact that the media world has recovered its sanity. European broadcasters, trapped in the financial straitjacket of falling advertising revenues and crippling debt burdens, have had a reality check and the shockwaves have rippled across the continent's biggest leagues. In Italy's Serie A, TV payments have fallen from £308m last season to £252m as the country's two pay-TV broadcasters trimmed their loss-making business models. In Germany, the Bundesliga took a 16 per cent pay cut, or a payment of £200m, following the bankruptcy of Kirch-Media, its pay-TV partner. English football has also suffered from the collapse of ITV Digital, which lost clubs in the Nationwide League £178.5m. (See Figure 9).

Sitting in his office at the league's Marble Arch headquarters, Scudamore is adamant that the Premiership's financial health will not be under threat when negotiations on a new three-year deal – the current one expires at the end of the 2003/04 season – start next month.

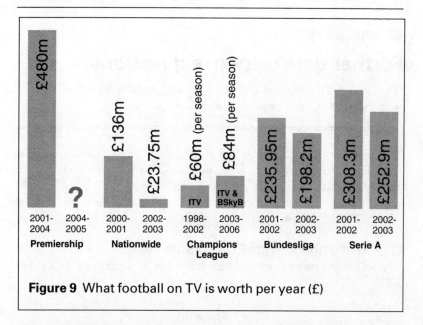

Figure 9 What football on TV is worth per year (£)

'It is a combination of factors that have caused difficulties in Europe. We don't believe those conditions apply in the UK and the Premier League because the competition is strong and therefore it's an attractive viewing proposition, the 20 clubs are committed to a collective selling strategy, and we have a healthy pay-TV market. It is not the same as what is going on elsewhere.'

It is true that negotiotiations in Italy were hampered by clubs selling their rights individually – the Premier League teams sell theirs collectively – and the German public has no appetite for pay-TV in a broadcasting environment saturated with free-to-air channels. However, there is no doubt that the sports rights market is in trouble.

Scudamore admits the sports rights market has 'burst', but insists the football industry should not be tarred with the same brush. Premium content is still commanding top prices, as shown by last week's improved £252m Champions League deal with BskyB and ITV, he says. 'I accept that the steam has gone out of the race for sports rights. But there is no evidence of that happening to premium rights.'

The focus over the next twelve months will be on BskyB, the pay-TV broadcaster that paid £1.1 billion for the rights last time round and has been the league's cash cow since the competition started in 1992. More than 80 per cent of BskyB's 6 million subscribers signed up to watch its exclusive live coverage of the league, but the company is dropping heavy hints that it will make a lower offer when it negotiates a new deal. This has led to speculation that the Premier League will set up its own subscription television channel if BskyB drives a hard bargain. Scudamore, who negotiated the previous deal, says the league will not be bounced into a pay cut, and going it alone is very much an option.

'We will start working on it [a new TV deal] in November, but we will not be slaves to any timescale. We will use time as a tactic to extract value. If we can extract value by putting together our own TV offering, then that is what we will do.'

He dismisses a report published by Sportcal.com which warned that a 'Premier League TV' channel with 3.5 million subscribers would earn just £264m per season, against the £419m from the current pay-TV deal, labelling it a 'pointless exercise … which makes a series of assumptions. It's just plucking numbers out of thin air'.

However, BskyB will also be making its own analysis of a breakaway channel, because the potential competition has withered away since the heady days of June 2000. NTL is emerging from bankruptcy, ITV is struggling with an advertising slump, and the BBC cannot afford a bidding war with BskyB. If the only bidders are BskyB and an untested breakaway channel, the contest may be over quickly. Scudamore also faces similar problems with the highlights package, which was sold to ITV for £183m but will do well to make its money back, according to executives at Network Centre.

However, the real problem facing the Premier League, and indeed BskyB, is Mario Monti. The EU's competition commissioner appears determined to shake up the relationship between football clubs and broadcasters across Europe. He has already coerced UEFA, European football's governing body, to sell the rights to the Champions League to more than one broadcaster per country. In the UK, this resulted in ITV and BskyB sharing the TV rights for the first time, in a deal which actually increased their value from £60m per year to £84m.

The prospect of doing the same to the Premier League could cause problems. If BskyB is told it can only screen 45 live games instead of the usual 66, the Premier League will cease to be the exclusive property of the pay-TV outfit, and BskyB will cut its bid significantly. In turn, the league will have to rely on ITV, the BBC or NTL to make up the shortfall by paying premium pay-TV level prices for the remaining games, which are around £5.5m per match under the terms of the current live deal.

The competition commission is already looking at the present BskyB deal, and EU sources said the UEFA case would be a benchmark for the investigation.

'He [Monti] said quite clearly when he presented the Champions League compromise that he believed it should serve as an example of how to solve similar competition problems with domestic leagues,' says Scudamore. 'We have to accept that sport has become big business, so the fact that clubs get together and sell the rights together, through the national association, means they are pooling forces to sell something.'

He points out that the Premiership matches were offered in three different packages – live coverage, pay-per-view and highlights – and were bought by three different broadcasters.

'The way we went about the process has been very transparent, and very pro-competitive. The actual outcome we also view as being very pro-competitive.'

Given all the pitfalls facing Scudamore over what promises to be a long twelve to eighteen months, it is the Premier League that needs to keep a level head this time.

Questions

1. According to the article, the chief executive of the English Premier League is confident about prospects for the forthcoming TV rights negotiation. Identify and explain:
   (a) *three* reasons why he believes difficulties for European soccer leagues do not apply in England   [6 marks]
   (b) one reason why he believes the overall downturn in the sports rights market does not apply to his product.   [2 marks]
2. Explain why BskyB is likely to believe it can negotiate a lower-priced deal for English Premiership TV coverage for the period beginning 2004 than it did for 2001–2004.   [6 marks]
3. Discuss the possible impact of EU competition policy on the English Premier League's revenues from TV.   [6 marks]

Q2 – At the races

The following piece is adapted from *The Guardian* of 26 March 2002.

Racing faces its £307m question

As the television rights deal between ITV Digital and the Football League started to unravel last week, some racing fans may have felt that the story holds a salutary warning for their own sport and its crucial relationship with broadcasting. Specifically, is there any danger the meltdown facing ITV Digital in March 2002 could be visited upon attheraces.co.uk in a few years' time?

Here is a company created by two major broadcasters that paid a huge sum for media rights – but now its media owners are threatening to turn off the lights and walk away, leaving anybody who thinks they are owed money with just a bankrupt subsidiary to sue.

At first sight, there are worrying parallels. ITV Digital is owned by Carlton and Granada, while Channel 4 and BSkyB are among the major shareholders of the attheraces consortium which agreed a £307m 10-year deal for racing's media rights nine months ago.

The attheraces shareholders agreed to pay all that money for terrestrial, interactive and internet pictures because they think they can get it back, and more, from exploiting the rights – just as ITV Digital no doubt did. Is their's any more of a realistic ambition than that of the ITV companies?

You can jot down on the back of an envelope roughly what attheraces need to do just to break even. Their outgoing rights payment works out at, say, £30m a year. On top of that they have the overheads of running a television channel and a hi-tech website, and they have to get it all back before they can make a penny. Attheraces has three main revenue streams. They have guaranteed rights income from effectively selling the pictures on to the terrestrial broadcasters, Channel 4 and the BBC. They also hope to sell them abroad. And then there is the betting.

This, clearly, is the big if: betting revenue from a live-pictures website and, above all, via interactive digital television. The attheraces.co.uk website has been running since earlier this year but realistically will not go large until Britain goes broadband. The interactive digital channel is to be launched on May 1. If both take off in a big way, all concerned in the rights deal – including racing, which gets a slice when profits pass a certain level – could end up rich.

But are these new gambling platforms viable? If you make a (very generous) assumption that attheraces can show a profit of 10% on betting turnover, which is around the level bookies look for, then to make, say £15m annually from gambling, attheraces need to turn over £150m. That is almost 10 per cent of what Ladbrokes manage, with 1700 betting shops and 40 years' worth of brand recognition behind them.

That is, as they say, a big ask. But interactive betting does at least have the potential to produce a healthy return. This is a major difference between attheraces and ITV Digital, which must rely almost entirely on subscriptions to cover its costs. As soon as sign-ups started to fall below target, its accountant ran out of red ink.

'Our deal is for 10 years, which makes a big difference,' Chris Stoddart, the chief executive of attheraces, said yesterday, 'and it is a mixture of mainstream and interactive rights, with major channels like the BBC and Channel 4 accounting for almost half of the spend across 10 years.

'We're selling to a mass audience, whereas ITV Digital is trying to use rights to sell a platform – and we have worldwide rights and worldwide interest.'

As for the betting side, Stoddard admits 'we've got to work bloody hard across the 10 years to make sense of it' but, at the same time, does not believe attheraces paid too much for the rights. The same view seems to prevail on the other side of the contract, where the 40 racecourses involved are already feeling the benefits.

This is another important difference between the two contracts. Racing, rather shrewdly, ensured that a signficant part of its income from the deal was payable over the first 12 months.

'One of the first things we did,' Stephen Atkin, the chief executive of the Racecourse Association, said, 'was to ensure that there were big first-year payments.'

Atkin concedes that the timing of the deal was fortunate. 'We think we sold at the right time,' he said, 'and part of that is good luck. We thought it was a full offer at the time we accepted it. But in terms of media value we were behind some other sports, and now we're punching our weight.

'It's up to us to respond to the challenge and raise the profile of the sport.'

Racing, then, seems satisfied it is not to go the way of Accrington Stanley. And if attheraces, meanwhile, must go all out for the next 10 years to make a decent return, well, welcome to the market economy.

Questions

1. Identify the *three* sources of revenue projected for attheraces.co.uk.
   [3 marks]
2. Explain *two* major differences between the deals, referred to in the article, done by the Football League and by the British Horseracing Board, which suggest that racing will benefit more than has soccer.
   [6 marks]
3. Explain the statement: 'That is almost 10 per cent of what Ladbrokes manage, with 1700 betting shops and 40 years' worth of brand recognition behind them'.   [4 marks]
4. Discuss the 'challenge' to racing referred to in the final two paragraphs of the article.   [7 marks]

Q3 – On the fly

The following piece is reproduced from *The Economist* of 10 November 2001.

Ready for take-off

British Airways is heading for record losses, but Britain's airline industry looks well placed to benefit from a bounce-back in the travel business.

At first sight, things look bad for Britain's airlines, The recession in the aviation industry, which started this summer, has hit BA particularly hard. It relies for nearly all its profits on business passengers crossing the Atlantic and flying other long-haul routes. Figures released this week showed that in October BA's overall traffic fell by 25 per cent, while its premium-fare business went down by 36 per cent. The outlook for this month is no better. Its financial results for the three months up to the end of September were equally bleak: profits in what is normally the best period of the airline's financial year fell from £200m last year to £5m. For the full year ending next March, BA's own stockbroker expects a horrendous £775m loss, though other observers think it could be much less.

BA's smaller rival, Virgin Atlantic, is also dependent on transatlantic routes, and is also struggling. It may soon need more cash from Sir Richard Branson's deep back pocket.

In these bad times, accounting profits and losses matter less than whether there is enough cash to keep a company functioning. BA admits it is dripping £2m a day as costs exceed revenues. But the airline has £2.4 billion available in cash, saleable assets and credit lines, which should carry it safely through a prolonged recession.

Most analysts expect real signs of recovery in traffic for mainstream carriers by the middle of next year, with a bounce back to previous peaks during 2003.

Aside from its stack of cash, BA is also well placed to forge an alliance with American Airlines: with the industry in crisis, regulators will be less severe than before about the competition objections. And as weaker airlines, such as Swissair and Sabena, go under, BA is likely to emerge as one of the three leading European carriers alongside Air France and Lufthansa. BA confirmed this week that it was talking to the Netherlands' KLM about collaboration on short-haul routes in Europe.

This week the British flag-carrier got a morale boost when it re-started Concorde services to America, with a chartered flight to take Tony Blair to Washington to meet George Bush and still get back to hold a war cabinet meeting the next day, and an invitation-only VIP flight to New York on the morning of 7 November. Both provided a public-relations boost to BA, which plans soon to ask the government for some cash compensation for the shutdown in America in September.

BA is looking forward to further good news when the government announces its decision on a fifth terminal for Heathrow. Observers reckon that it will get the go-ahead, with fewer conditions than might have been expected in better times.

Britain's other aviation ace is its lowfare sector, which flourished because the market was deregulated earlier than that in other European countries. Ryanair may be based in Dublin, but much of its business runs out of London's Stansted airport. This week it reported profits up 39 per cent and booming revenues, thanks to aggressive price offers which attract publicity and passengers. Last week Easyjet, which is based at Luton airport, reported a similar boom, thus giving the lie to pessimists who think that September's terrorist attacks have made everyone afraid of flying.

Both airlines are also expanding vigorously from new bases in mainland Europe. Britain's other big carrier (BMI better known under its old name of British Midland) is a private company which keeps its results to itself; but it is in effect a subsidiary of Lufthansa, secure in the mighty Star Alliance, and robust enough to weather any downturn. So as Europe's little flag-carriers fall, the prospects for British airlines get better and better.

Questions

1. (a) What is meant by 'recession in the aviation industry'?   [2 marks]
   (b) Identify *two* pieces of evidence mentioned in the article to justify the statement that there is a recession in the industry.
   [2 marks]
2. (a) Identify *three* characteristics of an oligopoly.   [3 marks]
   (b) Explain suggestions in the article that:
      (i) Britain's aviation industry became more contestable because of deregulation   [3 marks]
      (ii) the crisis in the industry in 2001 was likely to reduce anti-competitive regulation.   [3 marks]
3. The article suggests that the prospects for British airlines are likely to improve. Discuss the possible consequences for British airline passengers.   [7 marks]

Q4 – The sky's the limit

The big four

Where would you go to book your summer holiday? To a new MyTravel Megastore in Norwich or in Teeside, perhaps? Or maybe to Edwin Doran's Travel World in Twickenham?

The first is one of the travel agencies owned by the 'Big Four' tour operators – Thomson, MyTravel, Thomas Cook and First Choice, who control 24, 23, 15 and 13 per cent respectively of the annual UK holiday market of about 20 million packages (see Figure 10). The second is one of the UK's independent travel agents; Mr Doran happens to be chairman of CARTA, the Campaign for Real Travel Agents.

Thomson
Travel agents Lunn Poly, Caliers Pegasus, Sibbald Travel and Travel House are part of the same company as tour operators Thomson Holidays, Austravel, Club Free-style, Crystal, Headwater Holidays, Jersey Travel Service, Jetsave, Just, Magic Travel Group, QSL Villas, Portland Direct, Simply Travel, Skytours, Something Special Holidays, Spanish Harbour Holidays, Thomson Breakaway and Tropical Places.

MyTravel
Agents Going Places, Travelworld, MyTravel and Holidayworld belong to the same company as tour operators Airtours, Aspro, Bridge, Cresta, Direct Holidays, Eurosites, Jetset, Leger, Manos, Panorama and Tradewinds.

Thomas Cook
Thomas Cook travel agents are part of the same company as tour operators JMC, Club 18 – 30, Neilson, Style Holidays, Sunset and Time Off. British Airways Holidays and Thomas Cook Holidays are owned jointly by Thomas Cook and British Airways.

First Choice
Agents Travel Choice, Bakers Dolphin and Holiday Hypermarket are part of the same company as tour operators First Choice Holidays, Citalia, Eclipse, Flexiski, Hayes & Jarvis, Longshot Golf Holidays, Meon Villas, Sovereign, Sunquest, Sunsail, Sunstart, Unijet and 2wentys.

Figure 10 Who's linked to whom in the travel game? The make-up of the Big Four tour operators

It all depends on what you want. If your target is a cheap, mass-market package, then one of the Big Four's travel agencies is likely to be the best place to look – but don't expect them to give you impartial advice. Understandably, as vertically integrated firms, their travel agents would like to sell you one of their own tour operators' packages; indeed, one of the criticisms of Thomas Cook, whose profit performance was not impressive prior to their 2001 takeover by German conglomerate giant C&N, was that their travel agencies did not do a hard-sell for JMC, their in-house tour operation.

On the other hand, you are probably better advised going to an independent agency if you want a holiday with an independent operator, or indeed merely impartial advice. Mr Doran expects his staff, where possible, to offer customers three different holiday options, and he reckons that his shelves display brochures for 150 tour operators. Many of these are high-quality independent operations that are members of the Association of Independent Operators. They trust the likes of Mr Doran to sell their holidays, but most won't have anything to do with the bigger travel agency chains. At the same time, Mr Doran refuses to put the brochures of the mass-market operators out on the racks.

Of course, 2001 was not a good year for any holiday companies. World tourism as a whole fell by 1.3 per cent – around 8 million trips – the first fall for 20 years, and the biggest since mass travel began, according to the World Tourism Organization. The UK's Big Four were not immune from the downturn, and responded by making large cutbacks in personnel and in capacity. Their economics traditionally have always been rather strange, for example with a profit margin on each package sold often as low as 1 per cent. But the fall in demand may have brought some sensible realism into their strategies. Thomas Cook's new German owners have made clear that profits and efficiency, with margins a more respectable 4 per cent, are now to be the targets, and the other three are also becoming more concerned with margins and profitability than with sheer bulk.

The danger of a price war, however, is always there: 'if someone breaks rank, prices will tumble, and it could be disastrous,' one industry insider was quoted as warning.

Further consolidation in the industry is also felt to be a possibility. When Airtours made a hostile bid for First Choice two years ago, the takeover was blocked by the European Commission competition authorities. One analyst, however, recently said: 'The market in the UK is pretty cut-throat – you can see that in the wafer-thin margins. Putting Airtours and First Choice together now would not harm competition.'

Questions

1. (a) Explain the difference between vertical and horizontal integration between companies. [2 marks]

   (b) Give an example from the text which would illustrate horizontal integration. [1 mark]

   (c) Explain the potential benefits to a firm such as Thomas Cook of being vertically integrated. [3 marks]

2. With the four largest firms accounting for approximately 75 per cent of the UK holiday market, the industry would be characterized as an oligopoly.

(a) What do you understand by an oligopoly? [3 marks]

(b) Explain how profit margins might come to be very low in the industry. [5 marks]

3. Discuss whether or not the competition authorities should permit a merger between two of the Big Four firms in the industry. [6 marks]

Q5 – Setbacks

The following piece is adapted from *The Observer* of 7 October 2001.

Trouble in the skies

There is no doubt that this week's troubles at Swissair are only the beginning of further airline groundings to come. Thousands of staff cuts and loss-making balance sheets all seem rather remote to the majority of us. But when airlines start axeing routes and closing down, then many more of us are directly affected.

We could soon be back in the days before EU intervention when there were monopolies and duopolies on most major routes in Europe. This meant that, for most European capital cities, just British Airways and one national carrier offered tickets to each place. Although airlines were banned from price-fixing, you would often find return tickets to a city costing several hundred pounds sterling, and the two airlines involved offering fares within a few pounds of each other.

Before European airline deregulation, travelling to somewhere else in Europe was often more expensive than travelling to the US. After the EU broke the monopolies, new players such as Easyjet and Ryanair popped up offering cut-price, no-frills services. The result? When only SAS and British Airways flew between London and Stockholm, it was near impossible to get a seat for under £300. This week, Ryanair is advertising a return fare for £19.98; admittedly, this is a 'special offer', designed to encourage travel after last month's terrorist attacks – but similar bargain deals were available before the special sale.

But, however busy the low-cost airlines boast they are right now, the reality is that they are suffering too. Although their load factors might be high, the fact is that they are not making money, and there are likely to be casualties amongst low-cost carriers as well as the more traditional airlines.

There is a real problem here. If we don't travel, there are price wars – good news for consumers in the short-term. But then airlines go bust, prices go up, and many of us won't even have the choice to travel by air any more.

Questions

1. Explain what you understand by 'tacit collusion' in oligopoly. Illustrate your answer using an example from the article. [5 marks]
2. (a) Explain what is meant by 'deregulation' in the airline industry. [3 marks]
   (b) What evidence is given in the article which suggests that deregulation occurred earlier in the US airline industry than in Europe? [1 mark]
3. (a) Why are price wars most likely to occur when demand is falling? [3 marks]
   (b) Discuss the possible consequences for airlines and their consumers of continued falls in demand for air travel. [8 marks]

Q6 – Advertising agonies

The following piece is adapted from *The Guardian* of 24 August 2002.

Carlton and Granada get together

The two biggest ITV companies, Carlton and Granada, were accused this week of 'a merger by stealth' by a furious trade body, the influential Incorporated Society of British Advertisers.

'The ISBA said the plan [announced this week] to pool the two companies' marketing and programming divisions could lead to illegal sharing of information about advertisers,' said *The Guardian*. The 'depth of hostility' towards what is a virtual merger was underlined by advertisers saying they 'would not hesitate to complain to regulators about the potential power the combined group would wield'. According to government sources, the agreement is likely to prompt intense scrutiny from the competition commission.

The collaboration, which follows a failed merger earlier this year, is designed to improve viewing figures, lift advertising revenues, and deliver annual cost savings of between £10m and £15m. 'Coming shortly after the embarrassing collapse of the two companies' ITV Digital joint venture, and growing fears about their debt, [the news] helped bolster their flagging share price,' said the *Daily Express*.

Carlton and Granada were also believed to have expressed an interest in the television arm of the debt-laden Scottish media company SMG. SMG owns the Grampian and Scottish Television franchises and is 'understood to be seeking £300m or more', said the *Scotsman*. 'But in the curent climate both ITV giants are thought reluctant to pay those kind of sums.' According to the *Daily Express*, 'They were also concerned they would break regulatory constraints if they went ahead with the deal'.

Gerry Murphy, the chief executive of Carlton, says the company 'has to adapt – and quickly – to a fundamentally different environment in British broadcasting', according to the *Financial Times*. 'That means adopting a radical new approach to ITV's lifeblood: the big advertisers such as Unilever and Ford who together spend about £2.5 billion on television airtime. … Under pressure from a resurgent BBC, and growth at British Sky Broadcasting, ITV has seen its audience share slide to 22.5 per cent this summer compared with 25.7 per cent last year and almost 29 per cent in 2000.'

With a more innovative approach, Murphy hopes to take advantage of a slow recovery in advertising, and 'to sustain Carlton – and Granada – until they can finally agree and carry out a long-awaited merger. … The draft communications bill is due to liberalize media ownership rules and clear the way for the creation of a single ITV company', said the *Financial Times*. 'The whole effort is [also] designed to counter the competitive threat from the BBC and BskyB.'

Questions

1. What are the main sources of revenue for the BBC, the ITV companies, and BskyB? [3 marks]
2. Explain the major problems faced by Carlton and Granada, the two biggest ITV companies. [4 marks]
3. It is suggested that the proposed collaboration between Carlton and Granada would, among other benefits, 'deliver annual cost savings of between £10m and £15m'.
   (a) What is meant by 'horizontal integration'? [2 marks]
   (b) Explain how such horizontal integration might be expected to lead to cost savings. [4 marks]
4. Discuss the advantages and disadvantages to society of liberalizing media ownership rules. [7 marks]

Q7 – By land and by sea

The following piece is reproduced from *The Guardian* of 4 June 2002.

Ferries get stern

Cross-Channel ferries have found life tough since Eurotunnel opened and duty-free ended. But they have sharpened their act.

Left floundering after the opening of the Channel tunnel, then all at sea following the abolition of duty-free, Britain's cross-Channel ferries have found life on the ocean wave to be a stormy experience in recent years (see Figure 11).

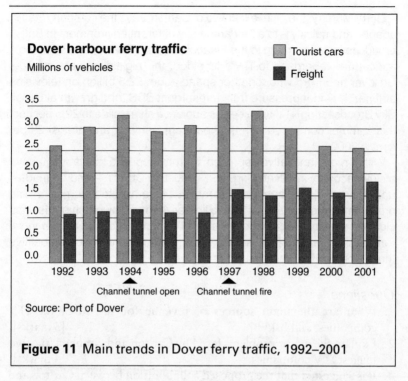

Figure 11 Main trends in Dover ferry traffic, 1992–2001

Hit last year by foot and mouth disease and thrown by the popularity of low-cost airlines, few seafarers can remember such sweeping changes in the industry. Among British operators, tempers have flared over subsidies for foreign firms which have made a competitive market even tougher.

Britain's biggest ferry firm, P&O, last month announced a widespread reorganization which will cut its fleet of ships from 24 to 17 and end services on several long, uneconomic routes.

With the minimum of fanfare, P&O expects to finalize a deal within the next few weeks to disentangle its Dover routes from Stena, the Swedish ferry network. P&O Stena Line, a household name since it was created in 1998 to challenge Eurotunnel, is deemed to have served its purpose and is to be dissolved.

The separation of P&O and Stena has received a mixed response. The Rail, Maritime and Transport union (RMT) has welcomed the fact that there are to be no redundancies at Dover. The RMT's national officer for shipping, Tony Santamera, said: 'We haven't fared too badly at Dover. Industrial relations down there have begun to improve and to a great extent, we're holding our own.' But others complain that the deal is too neat. One industry source said it was 'a complete carve-up – nice work if you can share it'.

As part of the reorganization, P&O is pulling out of the Suffolk port of Felixstowe, due to a slump in freight traffic on lengthy trips to Rotterdam and Zeebrugge, and selling its two ships there to Stena, which will run them from nearby Harwich. The effect will be that P&O dominates the 'southern corridor' between Dover and France, while Stena will have a strong position in the 'central corridor' from East Anglia to the Netherlands.

Tunnel threat

The shake-out comes after an eight-year battle to confront the threat of the Channel tunnel. P&O's ferry services director, Graeme Dunlop, says cross-channel firms have had to sharpen their act. 'We knew the tunnel was going to open and we knew it was going to grab a share of the market. Our strategy was to increase the size of the market, so we each got a slice of a bigger pie.'

Predictions of a catastrophe for ferry operators were misplaced, although there has been consolidation, both of routes and operators. Among the routes abandoned by big operators since 1994 are Dover to Boulogne, Folkestone to Boulogne, Dover to Ostend and Ramsgate to Dunkirk. Malcolm Dunning, the RMT's representative in Dover, campaigned in the 1980s to stop the Channel tunnel. He now admits: 'It was a bit of a waste of time. I gave evidence that the tunnel shouldn't proceed but growth in traffic has been phenomenal.'

P&O still sees underlying growth rates of 6–7 per cent for cross-Channel freight traffic, with leisure passengers up by about 5 per cent annually. The company has used cheap promotions, with fares as low as £1, to hang on to passengers.

Mr Dunlop says ferries have also smartened the on-board offering: 'Our perception was that taking the shuttle under the Channel was always going to be a fairly spartan experience. We've tried to mark out some difference. The whole outfit of ferries has been upgraded – a lot of them are built to cruise-style standards.'

On routes from Dover, P&O Stena's ships now boast Langan's Brasseries. Shopping options, once confined to booze, fags and perfume, now extend to wide ranges of compact discs, books and clothes. Mike Krayenbrick, Dover's general manager for ferries, says: 'Ferry operators on Dover routes compete hard with the Channel tunnel, particularly on day trips. We've seen very low fares because the value of on-board spend is such that ferry operators are happy to charge very little for the crossing.'

Dover harbour's traffic statistics tell a tale of two markets. Since Eurotunnel opened in 1994, the number of tourist cars passing through the port has dropped from 3.2m to 2.5m. There was a brief spike of growth when a fire shut the tunnel in 1997 but the decline accelerated when duty-free was abolished two years later.

However, freight vehicles are on the increase, up from 1.1m in 1994 to 1.7m last year, driven by economic growth.

Dover's government-appointed harbour board is making plans for expansion. It expects to spend more than £30m on two new berths for roll-on, roll-off ferries later this summer. This will take capacity up to seven ships, with plans to expand to nine within a decade.

But Dover's confidence is not shared universally – P&O is axeing services from Dover to Zeebrugge. Short-sea routes have tended to benefit from a decline in traffic on longer ferry journeys.

John Gummer, the conservative MP for Sussex Coastal, blames low fuel taxes on the continent, which have encouraged lorry drivers to drive rather than sailing directly to Holland and Belgium.

'There's a mismatch in the cost of transport by road,' he says. 'These boats provided an environmentally friendly answer. The government has got to take seriously the issue of minimum taxation in the European Union. If everyone had a minimum rate of fuel tax, these problems would have been minimized.'

A bigger headache for British ferry operators is competition from state-subsidized continental shipping companies.

Epic route

Seafrance recently launched the most modern ferry on the Channel, called the Rodin, which competitors complain was paid for by the French government. Seafrance is controlled by France's state-owned railway network SNCF. Another operator, Brittany Ferries, gets help from local authorities in Brittany and Normandy. To the fury of British ferry firms, Greek shipping company Attica this month launched an epic route from the Scottish port of Rosyth to Zeebrugge, taking 17.5 hours. Trading as Superfast ferries, Attica received aid from the European Union and the British government, which says it wants to encourage freight to take to the seas rather than roads. One industry source described the aid as disgraceful, saying: 'We feel it's a very dubious commercial proposition all round.'

Questions
1. Summarize the main trends in Dover ferry traffic between 1992 and 2001, shown in Figure 11. [3 marks]

2. (a) Identify *four* external factors which have adversely affected the demand for cross-Channel ferries in recent years. [4 marks]

   (b) Use economic analysis to explain how (i) consolidation of routes and operators, and (ii) improvement of on-board offerings might have enabled ferry companies to survive and prosper in the face of these difficulties. [6 marks]

3. Explain how relatively low taxation on fuel on the continent has affected the freight demand for cross-Channel ferries. [4 marks]

4. Discuss the arguments for and against government subsidies to ferry companies. [8 marks]

Q8 Data response question

This task is based on a question set by AQA in June 2001. Read the piece 'The economics of cricket' and Table A. Then answer the questions.

The economics of cricket

There are eighteen 'firms' in the cricket 'industry' in England and Wales (the first-class county clubs). The existence of some degree of monopoly is indicated by the existence of high 'barriers to entry', and it is in only rare cases (such as Durham in 1992) that a 'minor' county is able to gain admission to the county championship.

Unlike Premiership soccer, however, county cricket is not dominated by an elite few (such as Manchester United and Chelsea). There were six different winners of the county championship in the 1990s, including some of the less well off counties.

The 'price' of cricketers

In soccer, the wealthiest clubs attract the best players by paying the highest wages, and there is considerable evidence that dominance in soccer is strongly linked to wages (although there are, or course, other factors as well). For example, in 1999 Manchester United, the richest club, announced that they would be paying some of their players £50 000 per week. In January 2000, the average wage of Premiership soccer players was estimated at £400 000 per year.

There are about 400 cricketers employed in the first-class game in England and Wales, on an average of about £30 000 per year, with domestic players rarely exceeding £75 000. The rich counties compete for the services of overseas players, but prices are relatively high: Worcestershire paid one overseas player about £250 000 for a contract lasting two years. Provided the 'productivitity' of this player is high enough to enable the county to win some major competitions, the club regards this as money well spent.

Demand

A typical scenario in county cricket is a day's play attended by only a handful of members dozing in the pavilion. However, large crowds can be drawn to international cricket matches, and spectators are willing to pay relatively high prices for admission. There is, for example, invariably a large crowd at the Thursday or Friday of a test match in England, where the cheapest ticket will be about £25.

We can speculate that there is a range of demand conditions.

- Firstly, substitution. Films, computer games and the Internet are examples of substitute forms of entertainment that can satisfy the short attention span of today's consumer in a way that a complex game like cricket cannot.
- Soccer is the closest substitute for cricket, and today dominates the sports news virtually all year round.
- But cricket itself is partly to blame for its lack of appeal. If the England international cricket team were more successful, crowds would soar and income from soccer-style merchandising (replica flannels, sets of stumps emblazoned with county logos) would boom.
- Membership subscriptions and gate-money are handy, but income from television is particularly important. The current contract with Channel Four and Sky is worth £103 million over four years.
- Sponsorship revenues have been of considerable significance. Cornhill, for example, paid £28 million between 1977 and 2000 to sponsor test matches.

Table A Season ticket prices, 2000

Club	Cheapest (£)	Dearest (£)	Availability
Lancashire County Cricket Club	52	95	Readily available to members, who pay a one-off joining fee of £35
Manchester United Football Club	323	456	None available for the foreseeable future: fans advised to pay £15 annual membership fee and buy tickets for individual matches (range £16–£22)

1. (a) What is meant by the term 'monopoly'? [4 marks]
   (b) Distinguish between a firm and an 'industry'. [5 marks]
2. Explain how the existence of substitutes affects the market in which

cricket clubs operate. [5 marks]
3. With the help of a diagram, explain why the 'price' of cricketers is generally lower than the 'price' of soccer players. [8 marks]
4. Table A concentrates on factors other than elasticities. Explain how a knowledge of elasticities could be useful to help cricket clubs set ticket prices. [8 marks]
5. Identify and evaluate various ways in which cricket clubs might increase the demand for their product. [20 marks]

Q9 – Environmental responsibilities

The following piece is adapted from *The Guardian* of 21 August 2001.

Flight path to danger

Budget airlines have brought foreign trips within the reach of the many. Ryanair is threatening to overtake British Airways as Europe's largest airline within 10 years. But all this growth comes at a cost to the environment; the present rate of expansion is unsustainable.

Government forecasts suggest that travel from UK airports could more than double over the next 20 years (see Figure 12) and treble in 30 years. Air cargo is growing at an even faster pace. The question of whether to accommodate all this growth hangs over the air transport white paper, due next year. It makes the building of a fifth terminal at Heathrow look

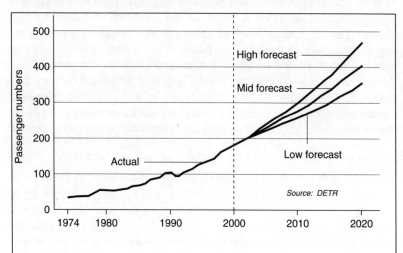

Figure 12 Passenger numbers at UK airports since 1974 (millions)

like the tip of an iceberg, since it would add only about 20m passengers on the existing two runways. The white paper has a 30-year horizon, by which time the number of passengers using UK airports could increase by 300m.

A decision on Terminal 5 is expected in the autumn. If it gets the go ahead, then runway capacity in the south-east would still run out within a decade. In deciding the amount of additional capacity needed, the challenge for government is balancing the benefits of trade, travel and employment with the costs of noise, pollution, climate change and the use of natural resources. The government plans to streamline the planning process (the Terminal 5 inquiry took five years and cost £83m). But it must be careful not to throw the baby out with the bathwater, by denying the legitimate concerns of communities under the flight paths.

The aviation industry is gearing up for a major campaign to meet capacity demands under the banner 'freedom to fly'. Organizations such as the London Chambers of Commerce and Industry argue that the UK's prosperity depends on it.

There are plausible reasons for believing that air transport expansion might facilitate growth in other sectors. It creates larger markets, promotes competition and fosters collaboration. Future growth sectors in the UK economy, such as pharmaceuticals, electronics and financial services, are said to be particularly dependent on air transport.

But there are downsides. Growth imposes congestion costs on the surface transport system, with people and goods getting to and from airports. Not all air travel is good for the economy. It extracts more spending by UK residents when abroad than it brings in spending by overseas visitors to the UK. The deficit is large and growing, already about £7bn in 1999. Growth in air transport is over-stimulated by a number of tax exemptions and subsidies worth an estimated £6bn a year. These include no fuel tax, no VAT on tickets or fuel, duty-free sales and cross-subsidy of airport charges by retail activity. If aviation had to pay its way, then growth would be much more modest, with passenger numbers perhaps reaching 240m by 2020.

Air traffic is a major and fast-growing source of noise and pollution. The increased volume of flights is outstripping reductions in noise and emissions from individual aircraft achieved by advances in technology. If the sector grows unchecked, then more of us will be exposed to annoying and health-damaging levels of noise and sleep disturbance. Health-based national air-quality standards will be breached around major airports. Aviation will make an increasing contribution to climate change.

A special report of the intergovernmental panel on climate change

(IPCC), the expert body established by the United Nations, estimated that in 1992, emissions from aviation already contributed about 3.5 per cent of man-made global warming. However, emissions from international aviation are excluded from the Kyoto agreement on climate change. Also, aviation fuel is exempted from taxation by international agreements that date back to the Chicago Convention of 1944, when environmental issues were hardly a widespread public concern.

The IPCC and the UK's royal commission on environmental pollution have both recommended at least a 60 per cent cut in greenhouse gas emissions by 2050. At the current rate of growth, aviation alone could be responsible for the total global sustainable rate of greenhouse gas emissions by the middle of this century, especially if new supersonic passenger planes are developed.

To put the development of aviation on to a sustainable path will require action at global, European, national and local levels. Emissions from international aviation should be included in the Kyoto protocol. The Institute for Public Policy Research has recommended emissions trading as a better alternative to aviation fuel tax. In the interim, an EU-wide emissions charge could help to curb pollution. Congestion charging at airports, through the auction of landing and take-off slots, would encourage more flights to less crowded regional airports, and rail substitution for short-haul flights. Airports should be required to meet national air-quality standards, and be subjected to tougher restrictions on noise and night flights. Noise and emission-related landing charges would encourage quieter, cleaner planes.

The choice we face is not between no growth and unfettered growth, but between sustainable and unsustainable growth. If the aviation industry is to develop on a sustainable path then it must take up its environmental responsibilities. Otherwise we will continue to use up our children's airmiles.

Questions

1. With reference to Figure 12:

   (a) Suggest why there might have been a slight fall in the numbers using UK airports in 1990/91. [2 marks]

   (b) These government forecasts were produced before the dramatic fall in the volume of air travel after 11 September 2001 and would undoubtedly be rather different if they were produced now. However, the process of producing high, medium and low forecasts is a standard one. Suggest *two* reasons why such a range of long-term forecasts is given. [4 marks]

2. Explain *two* benefits which are argued in favour of the projected

rapid growth in air travel. [4 marks]

3. (a) What do you understand by a 'negative externality'? [2 marks]

   (b) Identify *three* negative externalities which, it is argued, arise as a result of air travel. [3 marks]

4. Explain, and discuss the possible effectiveness of, aviation fuel tax and congestion charging at airports as a means of achieving sustainable growth in air transport. [10 marks]

Q10 – Rationing by price

The following piece is adapted from *The Guardian* of 18 August 2001.

Monumental expense

If you sweat your way up the Inca Trail to the mountain-top city of Machu Picchu this year, you will discover the cost of the trek has tripled. At the gates of the Taj Mahal, the admission fee for foreign tourists has sky-rocketed by 6000 per cent. Holidaymakers in Majorca could face an additional tax of £1.25 per person per night. And in Florence you may soon have to fork out simply for strolling through Renaissance piazzas.

It is not difficult to understand why. Every year we sightseers gather in larger and larger swarms. By 2010 the World Tourism Organization estimates there will be a billion tourist trips undertaken globally – compared with 663 million in 1999. The rise in air traffic volumes is even steeper, the economic pressure for new runways and terminals building all the time.

The problem is we congregate every summer in the most attractive heritage sites and wildlife reserves, generating lucrative business, educating ourselves about the world, choking native lifestyles, damaging buildings we have come to admire and spreading litter. Cities such as Venice, which hosted 11 million trippers last year, feel overwhelmed.

Increasingly, the solution of first resort is rationing by price, Galapagos Islands-style. Tourist numbers there are limited to preserve a vulnerable habitat and expensive tickets are in effect the mechanism for restricting the destination to a profitable upmarket clientele.

Poor countries with world-class ancient monuments are increasingly discovering foreign tourists as a ready source of revenue. Most of the money taken at Machu Picchu, it is promised, will be ploughed back in the form of improved services such as toilets and campsites.

Tim Murray Walker, marketing manager of the London-based travel agency Journey Latin America, understands the reasons. 'With huge increases in visitor numbers, the strain on the local environment and services warranted the new regulations and price increase to cover ...

the upkeep of the monument.'

The practice of having a two-tier pricing structure, favouring national residents but discriminating against foreigners, is becoming more and more widespread. In the Jordanian desert city of Petra, for example, foreign visitors have to pay the equivalent of £20 for a day's ticket to the ruins; Jordanians are charged £1.

Introducing entrance fees is even more controversial if the architectural treasure is a living city where throngs of tourists become a problem of crowd control. Florence is actively considering levying 2000 lire (64p) from each visitor entering the city centre.

The Balearic island of Majorca has an even more advanced scheme. Next year, if authorities in Madrid permit, a tourist tax of £1.25p per night will be levied on hotels and apartments. Funds generated will be used to upgrade the island's infrastructure and, possibly, to destroy unsightly hotels constructed in the first wave of package tourism.

The policy could significantly alter the character of Majorca's tourist industry, forcing out the cheaper, sun and sangria market and transforming it into a more selective resort. For a family of four, the new tax would add £65 to the bill for a fortnight's holiday. (Several years ago the Seychelles attempted to introduce a £75 environmental charge on visitors but gave up because of resistance from tour operators.)

The tourism industry is unsettled by Majorca's move. Hoteliers fear it will drive away a significant proportion of customers. The World Travel & Tourism Council accepts, in principle, that destinations can be degraded by pressure of visitors. 'It may be necessary to reduce the carrying capacity and increase the yield in order to maintain the viability of an attraction,' says Richard Miller, head of the organization's research and economics department in the US.

But he adds: 'If there's a need to put a price mechanism on, then the money must support the sites.'

That is because what infuriates tour operators most is governments creaming off profits from the buoyant tourist industry. As air travel and tourism have boomed, so the price of visas and airport taxes have risen way ahead of inflation. The money is usually channelled away from tourism into national treasuries for general spending.

Charities promoting ethical and environmentally sensitive tourism also doubt whether cash raised reaches those who most need it. Tourism Concern supports charging a 'fair price' for heritage sites.

'If entry prices are too cheap local communities will make no profit and have no incentive for conservation. It's a question of where the money is going,' says Tricia Barnett, the organization's director.

Questions

1. Identify and explain one desired and one undesired consequence of imposing expensive charges on, for example, visits by tourists to the Galapagos Islands. [4 marks]

2. Explain why Majorca's hotel owners, and tour operators, oppose the proposal to impose a tax on tourists to the island. [4 marks]

3. (a) What is meant by 'price discrimination'? [1 mark]
   (b) Explain why the authorities involved might have decided to charge foreign tourists much more than local inhabitants for a visit to the Taj Mahal or to the ruins at Petra. [4 marks]

4. (a) Discuss the case for introducing significant charges to visit world heritage sites. [6 marks]
   (b) Discuss the case for using revenues generated by such charges solely for supporting the sites involved. [6 marks]

Conclusion

Leisure is an increasingly important part of our lives. This importance is recognized in the inclusion of leisure as a topic for study by the examination boards.

Chapter 1 of this book explored the meaning of leisure, recognizing that leisure can be considered to be both a process and a product. It discussed the choice between work and leisure, bringing out the income and substitution effects involved when hourly wage rates change. It also introduced the main features of the market for leisure including the influences on the demand for, and supply of, leisure. The chapter concluded by discussing the range of activities that leisure covers and by outlining the relationship between leisure and the national economy.

Chapter 2 gave examples of leisure activities provided by the private, public and voluntary sectors and explained why they supply leisure. In the case of the public sector the importance of the concepts of merit goods and positive externalities in government decisions were examined. In the case of leisure industries that operate through the market, price elasticity of supply is an important concept. The chapter finished with two examples, illustrating that supply tends to be more elastic, the longer the time period under consideration and the more competitive the industry is.

Chapter 3 focused on the demand for leisure, discussing the main influences on the demand for leisure activities, why there is an inverse relationship between demand and price and the significance of price, income and cross elasticities of demand. In explaining why demand and price move in opposite directions, use is made of diminishing marginal utility theory and income and substitution effects. Price, income and cross elasticities of demand are explained using examples from the leisure sector. The chapter also discussed other elasticities of demand and the two main ways a firm can seek to obtain information on elasticities of demand, by analysing past data and market research.

In Chapter 4 recent trends in the UK leisure sector were explored, drawing on data from a variety of sources. It was shown that the leisure sector is growing in size. We are spending more on leisure activities and more people are being employed in the leisure sector. As well as providing data on the leisure sector as a whole, data is given for seven particular segments: tourism, air travel, restaurants and hotels, cinema and theatre, libraries and museums, television and home entertainment and professional sport.

Chapter 5 is the longest chapter in the book. It examined in some depth the characteristics, behaviour and performance of the different market structures of perfect competition, absolute monopoly, monopolistic competition and oligopoly. It also emphasised the particular significance of the models of monopolistic competition and oligopoly in analysing leisure industries and used these models to examine four particular leisure industries: air travel, television, spectator sports and package holidays.

In Chapter 6 the focus switched to the interrelationship between leisure and the national economy. Leisure is making an increasingly important contribution to both aggregate demand and aggregate supply. As the examples of the decline in tourism after the terrorist attacks on the World Trade Center in New York and the Commonwealth Games in Manchester showed, changes in the demand and supply of leisure industries have a significant impact on the national economy. Changes in the macroeconomy also have an impact on leisure industries. As the Chapter discussed, leisure industries are affected by changes in interest rates, fiscal policy and exchange rates. Leisure activities also influence living standards but as the chapter noted some may have harmful as well as beneficial effects.

The final chapter, Chapter 7, provided ten more data response questions. With only a limited number of past questions on leisure available, these should prove to be useful.

Index

Page numbers in *italics* refer to diagrams and tables.